blue
rider
press

IN THEIR LIVES

IN THEIR LIVES

GREAT WRITERS ON GREAT BEATLES SONGS

EDITED BY ANDREW BLAUNER

A NOTE FROM PAUL McCARTNEY

BLUE RIDER PRESS • NEW YORK

blue
rider
press

An imprint of Penguin Random House LLC
375 Hudson Street
New York, New York 10014

Yellow Submarine
Words and Music by John Lennon and Paul McCartney
Copyright © 1966 Sony/ATV Music Publishing LLC
Copyright Renewed
All rights Administered by Sony/ATV Music Publishing LLC,
424 Church Street, Suite 1200, Nashville, TN 37219
International Copyright Secured. All Rights Reserved
Reprinted by Permission of Hal Leonard LLC

Library of Congress Cataloging-in-Publication Data

Names: Blauner, Andrew, editor.
Title: In their lives: great writers on great Beatles songs / edited by
Andrew Blauner; a note from Paul McCartney.
Description: New York: Blue Rider Press, [2017]
Identifiers: LCCN 2016053859 (print) | LCCN 2016054722 (ebook) |
ISBN 9780735210691 (hardcover) | ISBN 9780735210714 (ebook)
Subjects: LCSH: Beatles. | Rock music—History and criticism.
Classification: LCC ML421.B4 I5 2017 (print) | LCC ML421.B4 (ebook) |
DDC 782.42166092/2—dc23
LC record available at https://lccn.loc.gov/2016053859
p.   cm.

Printed in the United States of America
1   3   5   7   9   10   8   6   4   2

Book design by Gretchen Achilles

For Jill

contents

A NOTE FROM PAUL McCARTNEY

The truth is that when we wrote our songs we hoped that one day a few people would know them and maybe even love them. Well, that certainly came true, and it is astounding to me to realize the extent to which the songs have reached people of all shapes and sizes in so many places around the world. People have told me how our songs have helped them through dark times, but I rarely hear detailed explanations of how they feel about them. So to me, that is what is so special about this book. Enjoy reading it.

INTRODUCTION

How few constants are there in our lives? Please stop and think for a moment: your family, maybe a couple of friends. What else? Not where you live, what you do, or even, on some level, who you are.

I have edited five anthologies before this one. Though each of them was satisfying, illuminating, I was ready to be done with putting these books together, but then, one September morning on a hill in Central Park, I realized there was something that has been consistent in my life, and in the lives of millions—if not billions—of others, through the past half century, and will likely continue to be so in perpetuity: the Beatles.

I was in the womb—literally—when the Beatles arrived at the newly renamed Kennedy Airport on February 7, 1964. I reckon that my mother's listening to the Beatles while carrying me might have had something to do with the cosmic draw that I have felt toward the band for as long as I can remember.

The Beatles were a powerful and joyful part of my youth and beyond, but there was a time after college when I felt as if I had lost them, for a spell. They went away. Or I did. And the silence was not deafening, but depressing. W. S. Merwin wrote of the way absence can go through you like thread, leaving everything you do "stitched with its color." Once I rediscovered the Beatles, I realized just how much the absence *had* gone through me, how much of almost everything I did *was* stitched with their color. If that sounds hyperbolic, it's not. And so, this anthology.

The concept is simple: Ask writers to write about their favorite Beatles songs, tell stories of what the songs mean to them, the how and why of it all. The title, *In Their Lives*, is an homage to one of my personal favorite songs—one that I first and so many times heard as a track on *Rubber Soul*, with its chocolate-chocolate-chip-colored cover.

We tend to hear about, talk about, certain things—be it baseball, or traffic—as the great democratizer, the fail-proof icebreakers, the common denominators, but the Beatles provide more common ground with almost anyone, no matter their age, gender, race, background, than nearly any other topic. Seemingly everyone, everywhere, knows the Beatles, and ever so many of us seem to have Proustian memories, meaningful and memorable associations, and experiences with them.

They have been our companions throughout our lives, from youthful, joyful innocence to the darker, more complicated side of things. It's axiomatic to say that something has become "the soundtrack of our lives," but in this case it rings true. For so many moments and occasions in our lives—happy or sad, at beginnings or at endings—there have been

Beatles songs there for us, that spoke to us, to those moments and those feelings, that put words and music to what otherwise felt unsayable. This unites us; it trumps and triumphs over our many radical, rageful, divisive differences.

And yet, given the body of work of almost unimaginable quantity and quality of loved songs, few agree on what the best is, what their favorite is. And therein lies the fun.

Across the universe of fans, the language of the lyrics—and the emotions and feelings that infuse them—speak to us: from "She Loves You" and "I Want to Hold Your Hand" to "Hey Jude" and "Let It Be," from "Yesterday" to "When I'm Sixty-four," from "A Day in the Life" to "Day Tripper," from Eleanor Rigby's "All the lonely people" to the "Revolution" you say you want. The list goes on and on and, almost impossibly, blissfully on.

For all of the resonance, there's also a built-in irreverence, an invention, an innovation, an introduction of new lingo, language, lyrics, which have become part of the vernacular, our collective, often unconscious repertoire, and our reservoir of phrases, emotions, concepts.

Written by essayists from ages eight to eighty, the stories in this book are arranged chronologically, according to the date of the song's release. By reading along that way, not only do we see the progressions and digressions, the evolution and trajectory, in the work of the Beatles, but we get a glimpse into their lives and, perchance, into our own as well.

ANDREW BLAUNER *New York City, September 2016*

IN THEIR LIVES

SHE LOVES YOU

ROZ CHAST

"SHE LOVES YOU" was released in the U.S. in September 1963, when I was eight—almost nine—years old. That song provided my first inkling that there was another world out there, one that did not include my parents, my relatives, my neighbors, my teachers, or my classmates—a world of carefree and attractive young people who did not worry about illnesses or money, and who did not care about homework or why one was not popular. The reason they did not think about these things was obvious: they were too busy having fun and being young.

When I heard "She Loves You"—that exuberant singing, like nothing I'd ever heard before—I became aware not only that that world existed, but also that I deeply wanted to be part of it. Before the Beatles, pop music didn't really register with me. I'm sure I'd heard it, but it didn't "reach" me. It was boring; a bunch of mushy love songs sung by icky guys with irritating voices and greasy hair and even ickier girls with bouffants. Ugh. Gross. A lateral move from the shackles of childhood to a different, but equally shackled, adulthood.

So, what was it about "She Loves You" that felt like an anthem of liberation? Perhaps it was that chorus of "Yeah, yeah, yeah," or maybe it was that thrilling "Wooooo!" Or maybe it was the Beatles themselves. I'd never seen anything like them. I watched the Beatles sing on *Ed Sullivan*, with their funny suits and haircuts, bouncing to the beat of their music and playing their instruments, and was completely, totally, in love. They were sexy, for sure, but not smarmy or creepy. I wouldn't say they were "wholesome," either, which implies a kind of rosy-cheeked, outdoorsy earnestness that has never, ever appealed to me. No. This was something else entirely.

That spring, the one after the Beatles were on *Ed Sullivan*, I was nine, and my parents and I went to Puerto Rico for a week. It was a school vacation, and since my parents worked in the New York City school system, they had the week off, too. I had befriended another nine-year-old only child who was staying at the hotel with *her* parents. Big shockeroo: we were both Beatlemaniacs. At some point, our two families were in a car driving to some tourist attraction. As the parents were chatting, she and I decided to sing "She Loves You" as loud as we could. We didn't know most of the words, but we knew when to sing the "Yeah, yeah, yeah" and the "Wooooooo." More than fifty years later I still remember how thrilling this was. I don't recall any of the grown-ups getting particularly mad at us. They were just baffled. This was for us, this kind of music. Not for them. And that was okay with all of us.

I had a record player in my room. There were no speakers. You opened it up like a suitcase, plugged it in, plopped your record onto the spindle in the middle, and manually placed the arm that held the needle onto the record as carefully as you could, because you didn't want to scratch the record. Anyway, my first Beatles record turned out not to be a Beatles record at all. It came from a discount store in our neighborhood in Brooklyn, and it had a drawing of four Beatle-ish hairdos on the cover. That was what fooled me. When I got it home, I immediately realized my mistake: these were instrumental versions of Beatles songs. There wasn't even any singing! Total rip-off. My first experience with false advertising.

When I was in third grade and close to the bottom of the social pecking order—not the very bottom, but, like I said, close—the four most popular girls put on a show for the rest of the class. They dressed up like the Beatles in suits and Beatle boots and Beatle wigs. Three of them pretended to strum guitars they had made out of cardboard. The fourth played a drum. I don't recall whether it was a real drum or made out of cardboard like the guitars. They sang a couple of Beatles songs in front of the class for our entertainment. One of them was "She Loves You," and when they sang "Wooooo!" they shook their heads like the Beatles. I watched them with a kind of envy. Everyone applauded. I hated to acknowledge it, but they were great.

My parents were not interested in popular music. Even Frank Sinatra and big band music were beneath them. And jazz? Don't ask. My mother played classical piano: Chopin, Beethoven, Schubert, Debussy were her favorites. Sometimes my parents listened to a little show music—songs from *Carousel* or *Oklahoma!* They liked Gilbert and Sullivan. My father loved French music. He was a French teacher and a Francophile. Sometimes he listened to Yves Montand or Edith Piaf. To their ears, the Beatles, the Rolling Stones, and the Mamas and the Papas all sounded identical. One of the more shameful fights I had with them as an adult was getting angry with them because they didn't listen to Billie Holliday or Ella Fitzgerald when I was growing up.

When I think about "She Loves You," and how much I loved that song, how new it sounded, and how happy it made me feel to hear it, I think about how much it represented the mirage of a possible future, one that was more joyful and more interesting than my lonely and borderline-grim childhood with its homework and tests and mean girls and stupid boys and parents who worried about everything and got angry over nothing. A promise that, in the future, things would be better, or at least I would have greater autonomy. And now that I am a grown-up, I can say that even though I'm not skipping along a jewel-bedecked street lined with chocolate-truffle trees while angels throw rose petals at me, it's definitely better than being a kid.

I SAW HER STANDING THERE

ALAN LIGHT

I CAN'T SAY FOR SURE what the first music I remember hearing was. I have some vague impressions of coming across the Allman Brothers' "Ramblin' Man" on the radio and being struck by the idea of being born in the backseat of a Greyhound bus, and realizing that there was a world out there I didn't really know about. My father and I would make up alternate lyrics to the chorus of "American Pie" (he drove a Dodge Dart at the time, so "I took my Dodge to the lodge" replaced the "Chevy/levee" rhyme, which was enough to crack me up every time). At home, my dad also listened to his jazz records, an excellent set of the post-bebop generation he had discovered in college, so I know I was hearing Miles Davis and Bill Evans and the Modern Jazz Quartet from very early on.

And I do know how things changed when my dad remarried, just before I turned seven. My mother had died when I was three, and I was wildly excited when Janet, my new mom, joined our household. Among the stuff that made the journey with this wonderful woman from her Manhattan walk-up to our suburban Cincinnati house were several dozen LPs. She was a former dancer, now starting to focus on writing about dance after working in New York City government, so most of her collection was made up of classical and Broadway recordings. But there were a few markers of someone who had gone to college during the transitions and turmoil of the sixties—*Hair*, Joan Baez, *Alice's Restaurant*, and, of course, some Beatles albums.

I can still rattle off exactly which discs she owned. She had *Meet the Beatles* (she would have been a college senior when the band landed in the U.S. and their first stateside album came out, and who could have avoided the curiosity?), and then a run of late-sixties releases—*Sgt. Pepper's Lonely Hearts Club Band*, *Magical Mystery Tour*, the White Album, the *Yellow Submarine* soundtrack. Living in New York as these came out, she would have witnessed the overwhelming cultural/critical response to *Sgt. Pepper* and then stayed on for the ride, at least for a couple of years.

It was 1973, only three years after the Beatles broke up, when these treasures entered my house. I must have heard of the group one way or another, but still it seemed that the music was being beamed in from another universe. I was transfixed. There are pictures of me strutting around the living room in my pajamas to "Yellow Submarine." I was intrigued by *Sgt. Pepper*—drawn in by the tuneful, music hall-style songs, yet unsure about the darker tracks—and a bit spooked by the oddity of the White Album.

But I was never less than delirious when it came to *Meet the Beatles*. The sheer joy, energy, youthfulness, and camaraderie of that record were impossible to miss, even (especially?) to a seven-year-old. Even the ballads were irresistible—their cover of *The Music Man*'s "Till There Was You" may sound sappy now, but to a kid, it just seemed sweet, and John's soaring, yearning vocal on "This Boy" devastates me to this day.

At the top, though, was "I Saw Her Standing There," a pure, driving rocker—a "potboiler," Beatles producer George Martin would call it. It was one of the first songs that Paul and John wrote together (though it was mostly Paul on this one) in late 1962. The recording—which took place about a year later, as part of the marathon twelve-hour session that would make up their UK debut album, *Please Please Me*—was intended to capture the raw feel of the Beatles onstage at the Cavern Club.

Maybe I had previously heard things this explosive on the radio, but not up close, on our own record player, able to play it over and over, and not in a way that connected with me nearly so intensely. The chugging bass line, stolen directly from Chuck Berry's "I'm Talking About You," made me dance with glee. I don't think playing air guitar was quite so pervasive in the early seventies, but I sure knew what to do. And even a child could follow the lyrics—"Well, she was just seventeen / And you know what I mean" . . . I didn't actually know what they meant, not yet, but the greater sentiment was still clear.

Mostly, though, was the sense of sheer delight the band exuded on this track. The iconic "One, two, three, *four!*" intro placed you right in the room with them. The fun they're having is obvious, infectious: the whooping and laughing, the punctuating handclaps, and the harmonies so bright, so perfect, while feeling so spontaneous. Just like in the song, my heart really did go boom.

I might not have understood exactly what made a song great or how a band worked or what was required to capture that sound on a record, but by the time Paul lets out the shriek that precedes George's guitar solo I knew I wanted to be near it. After discovering and exploring these records, and feeling the things that "I Saw Her Standing There" and all the others made me feel, I would never believe in anything else the way I believed in this music.

IN 2002, when my wife was pregnant, we went to Europe for one final trip before our possibilities for travel would become much more limited. While we were in London, I called in a favor, and we visited the EMI recording studios at Abbey Road. We stood and gaped inside each of the facility's three historic studios, especially, of course, Studio Two, the impossibly simple space in which the Beatles recorded about ninety percent of their work.

We can never be certain that soaking up the history of that one room in utero is what made my son, Adam, into a world-class Beatlemaniac, but we will always have our suspicions.

His Beatles obsession was not immediately apparent. The first music that Adam responded to tended toward vintage R&B (Ray Charles, Louis Jordan, Chuck Berry), which I suppose makes a decent amount of sense, given the irrepressible rhythmic charms and narrative shape of so many of those songs. My wife, Suzanne, would sometimes play Beatles albums within the day's rotation (the White Album was frequent dinner accompaniment for a while), but to no greater effect than anything else.

And then one day, when the boy was around three, I put something on (maybe it was *Revolver*, maybe *Abbey Road*—I'm really not sure), and Adam's head spun around like something from *The Exorcist*. "What is that?!" he wanted to know. And when that album was done, he wanted more. Then more and still more. It was, in fact, like a hyper-speed version of what I experienced with my mom's records.

His interest in all things Liverpudlian quickly exploded. His whole life, Adam has been a big fan of anything that comes in a list or a system (his parallel fixation at the time was memorizing subway maps from around the globe), so the endless configurations of which Beatle wrote or sang which song, and who played which instrument when, was immediately fascinating.

He worked his way through the four solo catalogs (who had any idea that there are actually about four hundred

Paul McCartney solo albums?), and studied the *Anthology* DVDs and footage of the *Ed Sullivan* performances. I stopped keeping up with the bootleg world a while ago, but my dear friend Sam, with whom I've shared Beatle fanaticism since the third grade, remains a serious collector, and he was all too happy to be Adam's connection when the child was seeking out rehearsals from the *Rubber Soul* era or alternate takes of "Revolution."

I took a very young Adam to see Ringo's All-Starr Band, and he even sat through Billy Squier's segment without protesting. We've seen McCartney several times, first at the 2009 show that opened the New York Mets' new ballpark. When I asked Adam what he most wanted to hear, he said "I'm Down," because that's what they closed the 1965 Shea Stadium concert with—and damn if Paul didn't play it.

Most exciting was bringing Adam along to the 2009 "Change Begins Within" concert at Radio City Music Hall benefiting David Lynch's Transcendental Meditation campaign, at which the two surviving Beatles played together for the first time in the United States since 1990. It was the first time I had ever seen them share a stage, and I couldn't believe I got to take my son.

In truth, it was almost too much to handle. Like many in my generation, I have a lingering sense that my peers and I just missed out on the Beatles, that we grew up in the shadow of the band and all of the revolutionary aspects of the sixties that they represented. We didn't get to experience the excitement of each new album as it came out; we just got to mourn when John was murdered. So seeing Paul and Ringo on a stage together was like a fever dream—and the set closed with the one Beatles song that got Ringo behind the drums; the night's only chance to watch the most celebrated rhythm section in history play together. Yes, you know by now that it was "I Saw Her Standing There." (Maybe this would happen with any Beatles song once you started paying attention, but it sure seemed like that one kept following me.) Fortunately, Adam fully understood the magnitude of the occasion.

By this time, he could rattle off all the songs, all the albums, including bootlegs, B-sides, and set lists. He was just like I was when I was twelve, except he was even better versed. And he was six.

This degree of his madness has waxed and waned a bit in the years since—he went through deep dives into the Rolling Stones, the Who, and various others before recently coming back into more full-blown Beatles mode. Most significant, though, at five, he began begging me to let him start playing the guitar so that he could learn to play Beatles songs. I made him wait a little while—I was just too afraid that trying at five would lead to disaster and disappointment and then he would never want to try again—but after his sixth birthday, he instantly took to the instrument. The first song he learned to play was, of course, "I Saw Her Standing There," and there has been no stopping since. And let me tell you that you have not lived until you've heard a first-grader rip through "Come Together" or "Helter Skelter."

———

THE POINT of all of this, though, is not to brag about my kid—although, as you can see, I'm not shy about doing just that. The point is that, for years, my son insisted we listen to the music of the Beatles for some part of virtually every single day, music that I had *already* listened to virtually every single day on my own, decades before. And though it sounds impossible, I promise you that I never once thought, *Oh, can't we put something else on?* In all of that time, over all of this exposure, answering a seemingly infinite number of questions about this one band, all that emerged for me were more and more layers of the Fab Four's greatness.

Sure, part of it is the emotion that comes from hearing the songs through my son's ears, watching him discover them for the first time. But beyond that, when you listen this often to the same body of work, you start to hear each part on its own: the nuances of each instrument, of every vocal performance. My God, these guys were good.

The great thing about having Adam fall in love with the Beatles was that it actually allowed me to hear the songs again—the songs as songs, separate from the history and the mythology and all the connect-the-dots stuff that had built up in me over thirty-some years of listening to and thinking about the Beatles. I could really hear the magnificence of a track like "I Saw Her Standing There," or even something like "What You're Doing," a song I had never paid that much attention to because it wasn't a major, influential work, though it is truly a breathtaking melody, constructed perfectly and gloriously performed. And then, certainly, to build back up all of the backstory and details and trivia, since that's part of what being a fan is about.

For the last few years, Adam has been deeply involved in the School of Rock program, and this semester, he's playing in a "Music of the Beatles" show. They mix and match the groupings of kids from song to song, so he's singing a few ("Don't Bother Me," "I'm Only Sleeping"), playing some bass ("Baby, You're a Rich Man"), and handling a whole bunch of guitar ("Baby's in Black," "In My Life").

I'm most excited, of course, that he's playing "I Saw Her Standing There." Not that I've even heard him practice it so far. "Dad, that one is so easy," he tells me, knowing that he can knock out a three-chord rocker without much effort at this point. But I know that, for those few minutes, watching my child on a stage bashing out the song that made me fall completely under the spell of the Beatles—and of rock and roll—will bring me as close to that initial level of pure, innocent joy as I can get. And it will remind me once again of the power of a band, and its music, that's still way beyond compare.

I WANT TO HOLD YOUR HAND

JANE SMILEY

IN ORDER TO TALK ABOUT the Beatles, I have to go back to November 22, 1963, when I was contemplating my watercolor painting in the brightly lit and many-windowed room of my ninth-grade art class. Someone came running in and told us what had happened—President Kennedy had been shot in Dallas. I felt a little bit removed because my parents had voted for Nixon, had always been Republicans. But mostly, I didn't know how to react, and maybe no one else did, either.

Friday was always an early day. My mother picked me up in our Oldsmobile Cutlass. My almost-two-year-old brother was in his car seat behind us. My mother was about to give birth again, in eleven days. Everything was somber. For the next few days, we watched the aftermath unfold. Yes, I remember the image of John-John saluting, but more clearly, because I was a horse fanatic, I remember the dark prancing horse with the empty saddle, his ears flicked forward.

Of course, I was used to television—we'd had a television

for nine years at that point, and I'd watched cartoons, base-ball, *Ozzie and Harriet*, *Roy Rogers*, *The Lone Ranger* (and every other show with a horse in it), but because I was afraid to watch the news (thank you, Cold War), I was not used to live events developing on the black-and-white screen. When my grandparents turned on *Lawrence Welk* or *Ed Sullivan*, I walked past and went up the stairs to read a book.

At school, I was a good student who wore light blue harlequin glasses and sat in the first row of my classes with my mouth slightly open (lifelong mouth breather). My hand was always up, but I did pay attention to the girls (only a few of them) who were looking at the boys (only a few of them) and the boys who were looking at one particular girl (dark hair, full figure). If anyone was looking at me, it was surely because I was growing so quickly—at the beginning of seventh grade, I was five-one. In March of ninth grade, I was six-one—so around the time of the Kennedy assassination, I was probably five-eleven or so, taller than all the girls and all but two of the boys. When I went to school dances (put on in the cafeteria), it was my job to stand in the corner and keep my eyes open. I understood that and didn't resent it. I wanted a horse, not a boyfriend.

My stepsister had graduated and left for college by then, but thanks to her, I was pretty up-to-date on popular music. I could sing along to "Runaway," "Take Good Care of My Baby," and "It's My Party" (I still can), though she was not a fan of Dicky Doo and the Don'ts. Susan had a steady boy-friend of the kind they had in those days—a fake husband who dressed well and took her to dances. She was short, cute, and sophisticated—her bouffant hairdo was always perfect. Mine was not—at some point during eighth grade, one of the other girls took me aside and coached me on how to sleep in my rollers, but I couldn't stand the feeling, and so my hairdo remained resolutely a mess. My mother, even though she had once been the editor of the fashion page for the local newspaper, had no advice—she was overwhelmed by the two-year-old, possibly dreading the one on the way.

Then came "I Want to Hold Your Hand."

I heard it first on the radio. There were two stations in St. Louis for Top 40 music, one K and one W. I went back and forth between them, late at night with the volume low, and of course they were playing the Beatles—there was something big out there, and it was getting closer. The first song I remember hearing was "I Saw Her Standing There." Since I had never seen a boy and a girl look happy or excited about their relationship (or a man or a woman, either), the ebullient pleasure of that "OOOooh!" took me by surprise—it reminded me of Christmas mornings, and opened up the possibility that my fellow ninth-graders (meaning that girl we all watched, who kept her eyes down during class, but who knew all the boys were after her) had no idea what love was about. Then I noticed "I Want to Hold Your Hand." "I Want to Hold Your Hand" was aimed directly at nervous junior high school girls—it had the same optimistic, upbeat pleasure of "I Saw Her Standing There," especially on that last rising note of "hand!" which practically lifted me out of my bed. It was a world apart from, say, "Mack the Knife," or even "Love Me Tender," which my aunt had liked in the mid-fifties and spoke to me of tight waists and poodle skirts.

At any rate, few of us in my class were paying attention to the Beatles—not that girl, and not my best friend, who was way too sophisticated for English mopheads and preferred Sam Cooke. (My best friend also had a boyfriend, but he went to public school and was already driving.) I'm not sure how the Beatles fans signaled each other before *The Ed Sullivan Show* of February 9, 1964, but we were ready and waiting when the show came on—we watched them disembark from the plane at JFK (the happiest thing to happen there in two and a half months), George with his eyebrows, John with his leather cap, screamers everywhere. On the show, the stage was bright, the Beatles stood up straight, they shook their heads. Their trousers were slender, they were smiling, girls were screaming and crying. There was a kind of neatness and panache about them that American singers didn't have and that seemed characteristically English. When the music stopped, they bowed suddenly, like toy soldiers, and that seemed alien and desirable, too.

Within a week, we started collecting Beatles magazines. We brought the magazines to school and kept them in our lockers. Between classes, we looked at one another's pictures and talked about the gossip—was John really married? Sad about Pete Best, but Ringo is so cute. Where is Hamburg? Most of the girls went for Paul. The intellectuals went for John, known to be the leader. A very short girl went for

Ringo, and I went for George. It was a pleasure to have something in common with classmates I had hardly spoken to before, girls who did not wear glasses.

It was not only that I went for George, it was that I became a George partisan, and on his behalf resented John and Paul, who seemed to push him out of the way whenever they had the chance. What caught me was his looks—the high cheekbones, the deep-set eyes, the jawline. There was something quite playful about his smile, too. You could tell when he was smiling because he had to, for the camera, but you could also tell when he was smiling because he just couldn't help it—his face would go from somber to joyous in a split second.

In St. Louis, we had a fabulous bonus, too—every day, on one of our stations (KXOK, I think), George's sister, Louise, would come on the radio and talk for five minutes about the Beatles. Louise lived in southern Illinois, in the coal-mining town of Benton, where Louise's husband worked as a mining engineer. Unbeknownst to George's avid fans in St. Louis, he had landed at our very own Lambert Airport in September of 1962 on his way to visit Louise. Louise's Liverpudlian voice on the radio and her presence nearby seemed like a special grace to us Beatles fans as we got more and more devoted in the course of the spring of 1964. But when the Beatles sang "I Want to Hold Your Hand," they didn't sound like Louise, they sounded like people I knew, especially when they cried out "I wanna hold your HAAAAANNND!" Right out of St. Louis, that flat-*a* sound.

Time passes slowly when you are in ninth grade, struggling through algebra and ancient history, writing out rough drafts of your English paper on *David Copperfield* in pencil and then doing your best to write a fair copy in ink. The teacher turns to the blackboard and notes are passed. Candy gives you just a glimpse of the cover of the new Beatles mag she got over the weekend, and then you sit in front of the school for what seems like hours, waiting to be picked up by your mom. The record companies and then the movie studio did a wonderful job of filling my idle moments by pouring out pictures, music, gossip, and information about the Fab Four. The songs and pictures went into my brain and stuck there. As I wolfed down Beatles material, I took in information about England and London and Liverpool, about the Beatles as the Quarrymen, the Silver Beatles, the changes in style and haircuts. I was already something of an Anglophile because of other objects of affection, like the movie I saw in the spring of 1964, *Tom Jones*, a revelation of style and energy that I have memorized and still adore because of *The Manual of Horsemanship of the British Horse Society and the Pony Club*, which contained passages like "How to describe a horse . . . 'Kitty,' a brown New Forest pony mare, rising five years, 13-2 hands without shoes, with a star, snip into near nostril, cornet ermine near-fore, sock off-fore, pastern partly near-hind and a stocking off-hind. Scar near-hind cannon. Branded 'C.D.' near saddle. Mane and tail on." Reading these pages over and over was like learning a foreign language—the Beatles helped me translate.

And there were events: I broke my arm in gym class, high-jumping, but kept riding the horse that I loved, which persuaded my parents that maybe they should buy that horse, and so they did, and so every afternoon I got a lift to the barn with a dashing equestrienne who was a junior, and we never said a word about the Beatles. I would run my hand over my new saddle, a Barnsby, made in England, much more exotic than the McClellan cavalry saddle we'd had to use at summer camp.

At the end of the summer, after "I Wanna Be Your Man," "I Call Your Name," and "She Loves You," when I saw *A Hard Day's Night*, I finally realized that the Beatles were alien, even George was alien, that they spoke in a dialect that had nothing to do with Missouri flat *a*'s and George didn't want to actually hold my ha-a-a-and. But by that time I was done for. Anything they wanted was fine with me. Watching *A Hard Day's Night* was a revelation. Yes, I watched it for the glimpses of George, the intellectual one, and for Paul's agreeability and for John's wit, but what I saw were the shots of the train, of Paddington Station, of the English countryside, of Wilfrid Brambell, who did not look like any man I had ever seen.

Later, when I got my own record player for my birthday, my musical taste veered toward singer-songwriters of the folk movement (Tom Rush, Joni Mitchell, Judy Collins, Ian and Sylvia). It seemed to me that the Beatles could not be played late at night in the dark because they would awaken my parents or the babies, or perhaps they were not for private consumption—they were for being onstage, running through the streets of London, pursued by crowds.

However, I continued to pay attention. George was only six and a half years older than I was. Paying attention to the Beatles in the mid-sixties was like sitting in the corner of the kitchen, watching older cousins or siblings try things out, learn things, get ahead of themselves, make mistakes.

After *A Hard Day's Night*, they settled back into being artists rather than a pop phenomenon. Along with my fellow screamers, I backed off: I watched, I paid attention. The Beatles grew up. I grew up.

I did collect all the albums, and I did see *Help!*, and I did keep track of George's facial hair. Then, in the fall of 1967, I went to college and took my record player. I lay in the dark in my dorm room and listened, over and over, to *Sgt. Pepper's Lonely Hearts Club Band*, to mysterious lines sung in mysterious ways, like "I read the news today, oh boy / About a lucky man who made the grade," or "She's leaving home (Bye bye)," which in 1967 seemed to me to represent everything that had happened in the three and a half epic years since "I Want to Hold Your Hand." Is there any time of your life when it feels as though you are physically experiencing the sensation of your consciousness expanding, thickening, taking on the outside world more than it does when you are fourteen, fifteen, sixteen, seventeen? The way that the simplicity of "I Want to Hold Your Hand" grew into the complexity of *Sgt. Pepper* echoed and represented to me the very sensation of maturing, of taking in the mysterious and making it your own, or, indeed, yourself.

I'LL BE BACK

SHAWN COLVIN

If you break my heart I'll go
But I'll be back again

THERE YOU HAVE IT. This is all you really need to know
about "I'll Be Back." The singer is consigned to his fate. He
cannot let go of his lover even in the face of rejection. This is
brutal, humble, naked honesty. I loved it when I heard it in
1965. I still do and I always will.

I was nine years old when *Beatles '65* marked some kind of
turning point in my relationship with the group. Maybe it
was the perfect storm of their writing becoming a little more
sophisticated combined with my ability to take that in, musically, lyrically, and emotionally. I felt I was growing with
them. The truth is that we all know a lot more at nine years
old than any of us give our children credit for. In 1965, when
I heard "I'll Be Back," I got it. I knew the song inside and out.
I knew all of them.

I ventured more deeply into "I'll Be Back" after I decided
to cover it during my tour in 1997. I sensed that it could be
slowed down and saddened up (my specialty). I was right. It

seemed to become even more mournful, more painful. Of course, at its core it's a sad love song of the first order. But I pride myself in wringing out every possible drop of heartbreak.

Allow me to scrutinize the chord structure. While I'm hardly a theory expert, I still know how essential the chord progression is to the emotion within the song. "I'll Be Back" starts with a minor chord, understandably. But Lennon and McCartney didn't let it go at that as they might have on an earlier album, and the song resolves at the end of every verse with a major chord, which seems counterintuitive given that the end of every verse also ends with the resolute sentiment of the whole tune—"But I'll be back again." And then, without warning, that minor chord takes us right into the next verse. The contrast is gutting. It's not an easy song, either. There are two B sections and a middle eight, which take us even further into this pain, but the payoff is always that crushing minor chord that begins each of the three verses.

John, Paul, and George are at their inimitable best in the three-part-harmony department throughout each verse. I always took the brilliance in that blend for granted until I grew up and learned better. The pedaled top note is pure genius. In fact, that's one of the reasons I wanted to do the song—just to be part of those harmonies.

Lyrically, I can't think of another heartbreak song as satisfying to sing as "I'll Be Back." I get chills every time I sing it. Every time. Not many songs hold up like that for me, singing them night after night. But not many songs are this perfect.

NO REPLY

ROSANNE CASH

When I came to your door
No reply

A HANDFUL OF WORDS, expertly woven into a fierce melody, reveal a plaintive story of crushing disappointment, framed by the strained and aching timbre of John Lennon's voice. I heard this song for the first time when I was ten years old. I got the album *Beatles '65* and played it on my little record player with its tweed case in my bedroom in Casitas Springs, California. It's a song about betrayal. He saw her walk in the door with another man. He's been watching her, but it's not creepy—it's heartbreaking. He is so full of desire that he can't help himself. The shock of finding that you aren't loved is the deepest cut.

In Casitas Springs in 1965, I was in my parents' bedroom, looking at my mother's clothes and trailing my fingers over the beautiful things in her long closet—the white chiffon and gold-sequined cocktail dress, the tweed suits, the silk blouses and capri pants—when the phone rang. I picked up the receiver at the same time as my mother, who was in the kitchen. She didn't hear me. My father's voice was on the other end. They spoke for a few minutes and then my father hung up. It's odd that I don't remember their words, but I remember the devastation I felt. Cracks in the foundation of their marriage were clear. I dropped to the floor. I couldn't hang up the phone. I sat and listened to the dial tone for several minutes, until I heard my mother walking down the hall, and then I quickly put the receiver back in the cradle. She walked into the room and acted as if nothing had happened.

The subtext of my own life was the same as the one in "No Reply": one of disappointment and longing. I knocked on my parents' door, and no one answered. My mother and father were not at home. Perhaps it's only now, a half century later, that I realize why those eight words held such power: they embodied shame and desperation. And the shame of desperation. Why is there no reply from the woman behind the door, who apparently once loved the singer? Why is there no reply from my parents? There is a terrible reason: someone else is in the house.

I wrote a song about the phone call I listened in on, twenty-six years later, called "Paralyzed":

I picked up the phone / You were both on the line. I must have conflated "No Reply" with my parents' phone call—same topic, same year—and worked it into a rhyme scheme and a dark, childlike piano chord progression. That's what happens; decades go by while songs are forming. "Paralyzed" isn't nearly as good a song as "No Reply," but my reach far exceeded my grasp at that point in my life as a songwriter and I was reaching for "No Reply."

In the bridge (or "middle eight," as the Beatles called it), the musical and vocal burst of intensity that happens when Lennon sings about seeing the light is like a splash of cold water in the face. He sees she is at home; there is a light, and her face is at the window.

Romantic betrayal is a sophisticated concept for a ten-year-old. What do promises mean if they are nullified by sexual restlessness?—something beyond my understanding in 1965. The song was mysterious. Betrayal was incomprehensible, but thrilling and dark. There was a roiling inner world behind the stoic facades, and that world could be the doorway to art and music. It might be a door I could walk through.

But "No Reply" is a song, not a short story or a cautionary tale or a letter to an advice columnist. The heartbreak in the words isn't separate from the infrastructure of the lyric form, nor is it detached from the melody, and, even harder to pull off, it is of a piece with Lennon's vocal performance. Ray Charles said that singers were better at fifty than at twenty-five, because a whole life showed up in the voice at fifty, but John Lennon was nine days shy of turning twenty-four years old when he recorded "No Reply." Just this once Ray was wrong.

In traditional pop songs, the title of the song would be used to dramatic effect in the chorus, to drive the topic home, but here the title is not used in a standard chorus—a really interesting musical choice. "No reply" is the third line of the song, and it's not sung again until the last line of the middle eight. The payoff, however, is at the end of the song, when "No reply" is keened twice—and *keening* is the only proper word to describe the pleading in Lennon's voice. Keening is the sound that escapes from the broken heart.

"No Reply" is a two-minute-and-fifteen-second master class in songwriting and lyrical economy, in which the most intense feelings are expressed in the fewest possible words.

Lennon's howl that he is going to die is the denouement of the emotional arc. He says it twice in the middle eight. It has the stark intensity of Hank Williams's line "I'm so lonesome I could cry." Or my dad's "I walk the line": plaintive to the point of transcending the meaning. The life that shows up in the voice is made of choices.

I am often a guest teacher in various college songwriting classes, and I find that many young writers want to show off their poetic ingenuity with complicated and clever lyrics that overuse adjectives and nature metaphors, all for the purpose of a vague and grand theme: Love, Loss, Pain. The problem is that they forget people, and real time and place, and the "furniture" in the scene. In "No Reply," the window, the door, the phone, the couple, the person who answered the phone, are all part of the same tapestry. It's not a new story. But the specificity—the clean capture of a normal scene—gives it soul, and, as is always the case in a great work, the personal becomes universal. Everyone has had their moment at the doorstep, and if they haven't, they will.

And there's the principle of songs that become part of the permanent record of our musical consciousness: truth isn't dependent on fact. Even though the song is credited to Lennon and McCartney, it's widely accepted that John wrote the song. Shortly before he died in 1980, Lennon said in an interview, "I had that image of walking down the street and seeing her silhouetted in the window and not answering the phone, although I never called a girl on the phone in my *life*. Because phones weren't part of the English child's life."

Lennon constructed a scene and created characters to fit an existing emotional template. Some might say there is no great truth in "No Reply," that it's just a catchy pop tune, cleverly arranged, sung by a riveting vocalist. Oh yes. That, as well.

Eventually, we stop knocking. We stop calling. We receive the message. Maybe we come back later, after years have gone by and feelings are more moderated and maturity provides perspective.

After the first dozen or so times I played *Beatles '65* all the way through on my tweed-case record player, I started to change the sequence. I played track one, "No Reply," and then picked the needle up, skipped over "I'm a Loser," "Baby's in Black," and "Rock and Roll Music," and set the needle down on track five, "I'll Follow the Sun."

I've returned to "No Reply" in every stage of my life. You develop a relationship with a song over a half century. The early years are flush with passion, strong territoriality, and a slight confusion. The middle years are a little numb and there isn't a lot of gratitude. The hallmark of my current phase is benevolent agitation. And love. I love the girl who cheated, I love the boy who had his heart broken. I love myself as I was on both sides of the door. The sequence of events is switched, however: I nearly died, then I saw the light. But I'm still reaching for "No Reply."

I'm a Loser

GERALD EARLY

I LIVED IN AN ENVIRONMENT where a good many people loathed "I'm a Loser," and the Beatles as well. I knew the song because my mother loved listening to AM radio. (She still does.) The AM radio she listened to played the latest popular music (in this instance, rock and roll, rockabilly, pop, and rhythm and blues), while providing the time of day on a regular basis, news on the hour, updates about community events, information programs especially offering legal advice, and, on African American stations, lots of Christian preaching. (There were also, on black radio, ads about joining the NAACP, and using Dixie Peach and Royal Crown hair products, Lydia E. Pinkham's tonic, and skin whiteners, which, I think, my mother found rather comforting because of their "racial" familiarity.) This made AM radio a combination of a bulletin board, a self-help center, a site of spirituality, as well as a source of entertainment that capitalized on being current. At the hub of this swirling mass of commercial connectivity was the personality disc jockey with his

agile doggerel, pitchman's smarminess, hip loquacious-
ness, parental concern, and toastmaster authority. He was,
in some respects, the king of social knowledge and communication. (I knew of only two women DJs when I was young,
both of whom were African American, Louise Williams
and Mary Mason, who both played gospel music on Sundays. Ms. Mason eventually went on to become a radio talk
show host.)

As a kid, I often enjoyed radio as much as and sometimes
more than watching television. I would sit on the front steps
of someone's house with some friends and a transistor radio
or go to some nearby park with one of my sisters to listen
together. Those moments combined the intimacy of a parlor
with the vast, wired excitement of an urban cosmos. AM
radio made its listeners provincial, homebound, almost sequestered. Although rooted in something very local, rooted
very much in a place, I also felt hip and sophisticated, as if I
were part of something larger, a member of my cohort's taste
community. AM radio possessed the amazing contradictory
power of making its listeners both capacious and narrow at
the same time. That was the meaning of its ability to con-
nect people with music and with each other.

It was this sense of connection that AM radio evoked
that made white teenage rock and pop music singularly so
attractive to me, even seductive. While many of my black
childhood friends dismissed much of white pop and rock
as corny—if there was anything the black people around me
felt that blacks did far better than whites, it was making

music and dancing—white youth music was for me exotic but also the sound of the mainstream. To know this music, to appreciate it, gave me, in some strange way, total access to my culture, to my society—in effect, total access to my own life. I heard a great deal more of it growing up than most of my black friends did, but probably considerably less than the average white kid, because I did, after all, have to juggle two worlds and stay true to one of them.

Race divided AM radio as it did much else in American life. There were two black radio stations that my family listened to: WDAS and WHAT, the latter being black-owned; and there was the major white Top 40 station, WIBG, called "Wibbage" by its DJs. I was never quite sure why my mother chose to listen to both the black and white stations, what purpose she may have had in mind about what she wanted my sisters and me exposed to. I was always uncertain about whether her choice of radio stations in fact had anything to do with her children, as she was so seemingly indifferent to our musical taste and so dispassionate about her own. On some mornings, my mother turned on WDAS, on other mornings WIBG, and on weekends, it was usually WHAT. I remember some of the DJs very well: Georgie Woods (the Guy with the Goods and the King of Rock and Roll), Jimmy Bishop (JB the DJ), Butterball, Kay Williams, and John Bandy, known as Little Lord Fauntleroy, on WDAS; Hy Lit, Frank X. Feller, and Joe Niagara (the Rockin' Bird) on WIBG; and Sonny Hopson (the Mighty Burner) on WHAT. And there was Jerry Blavat (the Geator with the Heator, the Boss with the

Hot Sauce), who made a name for himself as a teenage dancer on *American Bandstand* in the 1950s and then became a record promoter and later a popular rock and roll DJ who played a lot of black music on WCAM, a station out of Camden, New Jersey. A lot of black kids including my sister listened to his late-night show because he played very hip oldies. Blavat, a teen idol for blacks and whites, went on to host a television teen dance show. It was in this aural world of patter and platter that I learned the most about popular music and where I felt the music most deeply. (I learned from television variety shows, too—Dinah Shore, Andy Williams, Perry Como, Mitch Miller, Vic Damone's *The Lively Ones*, Sammy Davis Jr., Bing Crosby, Pat Boone—but that was mostly, but not exclusively, music for adults. There were also the television music shows for the young, like *Hootenanny, Shindig!, Hullabaloo, The Lloyd Thaxton Show, American Bandstand*, and others, which I watched religiously, but television presented youth music in another context that altered its authenticity.) Radio is the key here because that was this music's true medium, where the music seemed to exert its greatest pull on the imagination and the emotions, and I associate all my memories of the Beatles with AM radio. Growing up, I never owned a Beatles 45. What I did not realize while listening to "I'm a Loser" on the radio was that the song was never a single.

But I suppose music during this period of the 1960s was about the racial divide that was there but was being crossed, about a racial divide that was distinct and pronounced, and a racial divide that was blurred. "The Twist," number one on the pop charts in 1960 and 1962, was the most popular rock and roll tune of my pre-Beatles youth and the song that launched all the teenage dance crazes: the Monkey, the Stroll, the Stomp, the Boogaloo, the Swim, the Jerk, the Mashed Potato, the Crossfire, and the like. (The fact that black performers like Smokey Robinson and the Miracles with "Mickey's Monkey" and Major Lance with "The Monkey Time," both in 1963, popularized a black dance called the Monkey, a term that was often used as a racial insult, seems odd in retrospect.) "The Twist," composed and originally performed by R&B singer Hank Ballard, was covered by Chubby Checker (Ernest Evans), a black teenager who lived in my neighborhood and worked at a poultry store in the Italian Market on Ninth Street. (My oldest sister dated Ernest's middle brother, Tracy, and I went to elementary school with his youngest brother, Spencer, which was as close as any of us came to the celebrity culture of the moment.) Checker was a crossover sensation, as was "The Twist." He was promoted heavily by Dick Clark of *American Bandstand*, a program that was shot in a studio in West Philadelphia from 1952 to 1964. (The story goes that Clark's wife gave Evans the name of Chubby Checker, its bow to Fats Domino being obvious.) All the Italian kids in the neighborhood loved Checker, as did the black kids. I was so young at the time, so inexperienced and unknowledgeable about the ways of race in the world, and in some ways so protected from it by many of the black adults—and some of the white adults— around me that I thought this merging of these two very different taste communities was common, that it happened all the time, that everyone liked everyone else's music. I did not understand this cultural détente for what it was: a moment that concealed as much black anger and anguish as it revealed white privilege and power.

Checker went on to appear in two cheap teenploitation movies, *Twist Around the Clock* (1961) and *Don't Knock the Twist* (1962), that did well with young audiences, black and white. Although the black stations rarely played white artists (exceptions included Dusty Springfield, the Righteous Brothers, Bobby Darin, and Vince Guaraldi), WIBG, the powerhouse white rock station, did play black music, especially Motown, and black performers like Ray Charles, Shirley Ellis ("The Nitty Gritty" and "The Name Game"), Jan Bradley ("Mama Didn't Lie"), Aretha Franklin, Roy Hamilton, Billy Stewart ("Summertime" and "I Do Love You"), Jerry Butler, the Impressions, Gene McDaniels, the Shirelles, Sam Cooke, and the great Brill Building stuff by the Drifters and Ben E. King, along with the white pop music of the day.

From November 1963 to January 1965, *Billboard*, the music industry "bible," did not publish a separate black music or R&B chart, because the pop chart had so much black music on it. This fusion of black and white commercially would never happen again. (The other major industry publication, *Cash Box*, still ran its R&B charts during this period.) American music, briefly, had reached a sort of racial equilibrium. "I'm a Loser," released in Britain on the album *Beatles for Sale*, and in the United States on *Beatles '65*, came at the very tail end of this merger period. It is the common critical view that the British Invasion re-racialized the American pop charts by sharply dividing black and white taste again. British pop re-inscribed white teen taste. I do not recall any black kid I grew up with who liked the Beatles. (This changed when I got to college in the early 1970s: *Abbey Road* was very popular among my black classmates, particularly "Come Together.") It was not a way to score points or gain status among my black peers by in any way expressing an appreciation of white performers or white pop music. There were exceptions to this: Dusty Spring-field, Tom Jones, and the Righteous Brothers were white per-formers who were popular with blacks during my youth. But there were other exceptions, too, among the adults: Frankie Laine's rendition of the theme song from the TV western *Rawhide* was very well regarded. Laine, Rosemary Clooney, Dean Martin, Frank Sinatra, and Peggy Lee were some of the white singers I heard the black adults around me speak of with respect and admiration. But for black folk, no one could match Ray Charles or Aretha Franklin or Mahalia Jackson or Nat King Cole. Yet the racial politics of taste are a bit more complicated than many think and the average black person at this time, through television and the pre-rock days of radio, was exposed to more white music than even he or she knew.

I remember very well much of the white music I heard on WIBG: Roger Miller ("Dang Me," "King of the Road," and "Chug-a-Lug"), Bobby Rydell ("Volare"), Frankie Avalon, the Everly Brothers ("All I Have to Do Is Dream" and "Cathy's Clown"), Jan and Dean ("Surf City," "Ride the Wild Surf," and "The Little Old Lady from Pasadena"), the Shangri-Las

("Remember [Walking in the Sand]" and "Leader of the Pack"), the Four Seasons (the one white group that most of my black friends liked because of Frankie Valli's falsetto), Ricky Nelson, Johnny Horton ("The Battle of New Orleans"), Roy Orbison, Charlie Rich ("Lonely Weekends"), Gary Lewis and the Playboys ("This Diamond Ring"), Gene Pitney ("Only Love Can Break a Heart" and "It Hurts to Be in Love"), Barry McGuire ("Eve of Destruction"), Del Shannon ("Runaway" and "Little Town Flirt"), the Rooftop Singers ("Walk Right In"), Barry Sadler ("The Ballad of the Green Berets"), and more. Add to this movie themes and songs that became popular hits, such as Elmer Bernstein's theme from *The Magnificent Seven*, Henry Mancini's "Days of Wine and Roses" and "Moon River," Dimitri Tiomkin and Paul Francis Webster's "The Green Leaves of Summer" from John Wayne's *The Alamo*, John Barry and Newley/Bricusse's "Goldfinger," sung earthshakingly by Shirley Bassey, and Manos Hadjidakis's "Never on Sunday." So "I'm a Loser" came at the end of the racial pop merger and I heard it in this particular swirl of white AM pop music.

When the Beatles first took the United States by storm in 1964, I thought of them as playing white-girl music. I had this impression not only because of the crush of screaming girls who attended their concerts and crashed their public appearances but because, when I collected my fees on Saturday mornings during my days as a delivery boy for *The Philadelphia Inquirer*, I would see adolescent white girls, in their pajamas, cooing and giggling in their parlors over "I Want to Hold Your

Hand" and "She Loves You" while I waited in the doorway to be paid. (More than half my route went through the Italian portion of my neighborhood.) But there was something else that intensified this feeling: during this period, the teenage or slightly postadolescent white girl had become a kind of cultural icon with television shows such as *The Patty Duke Show* (1963–66); "Karen," which was one segment of a ninety-minute comedy anthology called *90 Bristol Court* (1964–65); *Gidget*, with Sally Field (1965–66); Tuesday Weld as Thalia and Sheila James as Zelda in *The Many Loves of Dobie Gillis* (1959–63); Kelly (Noreen Corcoran) in *Bachelor Father* (1957–62); and Shelley Fabares in *The Donna Reed Show* (1958–66). In addition, there were movies like *Gidget*, with Sandra Dee (1959); *Gidget Goes Hawaiian* (1961) and *Gidget Goes to Rome* (1963); *Tammy Tell Me True* (1961) and *Tammy and the Doctor*, with Sandra Dee (1963); and the appealing *The World of Henry Orient* (1964), about teenage girls with a crush on a pompous classical pianist. And then there were *Archie* comics, which featured probably the two most famous white teen girls in American popular culture: Betty and Veronica. My sisters loved those comics. I remember feeling a bit uneasy about being a huge fan of *The Patty Duke Show* (in part, because my sisters were) and "Karen," thinking perhaps, as a black boy, I was not supposed to like them, especially as these shows promoted the Hollywood version of the white pop music of the period (I first saw Chad and Jeremy lip-synching to "A Summer Song" and "Yesterday's Gone" on an episode of *The Patty Duke Show*, for instance), particularly surf music, as so many movies with white adolescent or postadolescent girls were beach movies. Beach movies, on the whole, felt foreign to me, and I rarely watched them, largely because of their audience, which was made up mostly of white girls. Neighborhood movie houses were also racially segregated at the time—unofficially in Philadelphia—and the black movie theaters I attended rarely showed surf movies. (The black kids I knew almost seemed insulted by them.) The white ones always did. Yet the kooky white-girl image had not only a certain attractiveness but a kind of identification for me at that time, as I thought the awkwardness and spunk mirrored my own. In a way, these girls were oddly inspirational, as they always seemed to be working against the kindly assumption of low expectations, and their vulnerability could make normal interactions menacing. I felt both keenly. White girls were certainly a powerful component in how I thought about the American teenager, but the sexism in the culture generally made it hard to take them seriously or to understand their desires and ambitions beyond marriage. The racism in the culture made me wary of them. At any rate, I initially thought of the Beatles as being intricately tied to this sort of "girl" thing.

This meant that the Beatles' appeal was for me to the wrong color and the wrong gender. "Them pussy-assed white boys makin' a mint makin' dumb records for them silly-assed white girls," was the way my barber put it, and all his black patrons expressed their agreement. But 73 million people—the biggest television audience of the time—watched the Beatles perform on *The Ed Sullivan Show* in February 1964 and they were not all girls and they were not all white, either. My family was among the watchers. They came away singularly unimpressed.

I liked the band's songs almost instantly, in part because I had heard so much white pop and teen music on WIBG that favorably impressed me, so that the sound was not foreign or alien to me. I understood it to be "white"—or ofay, to use the term of the day—music, and I understood that it sounded "white," and even understood why that particular sound had an appeal to whites; in part, because most blacks would not be attracted to it. (Interestingly, most blacks I knew growing up thought white music was the *absence* of the typological features of black music.) But I was nearly the same age as most of the people who made up the audience for the Beatles music, and much of its appeal to me was the same as its appeal to them: the music expressed my own urgings and preoccupations; it was catchy in the way good pop tunes should be; it was hip, notably and refreshingly distinct from other teen pop music. It stood out in the morass of white AM pop. Also, their music did something that I found liberating: it freed teen music from being dance music.

The amplified guitars (similar to, yet different from, the electric guitars of Chuck Berry and Bo Diddley), the whiny harmonica of "Please Please Me," for instance, and "I'm a Loser" underscored the music's simplicity and its homage to folk music, which, at this time, was enjoying a considerable revival. This connection to folk music was crucial, as James Miller points out, to the Beatles' success: "Both genres

welcomed, indeed highly prized, the creativity of frank amateurs; both rock and folk were do-it-yourself formats that inspired many listeners to start bands of their own; finally, both
rock and folk were simple enough musical forms that even
teenagers could, without much practice, successfully approxi-
mate the sounds they heard on their radios and record players."* There was something about the accessibility of the
Beatles that made their music an awakening, as if saying,
"Take heart." Theirs was schoolboy music, appropriately
enough, as they were themselves art school dropouts. I did not
know this at the time but felt it intuitively about this music.
But this was schoolboy music with a difference, as the school-
boys wrote, played, and conceived the music, which made it
different from the schoolboy art of doo-wop or the boy-and-
girl singing groups of the 1960s that sang other people's music. The Beatles made me aware for the first time of who
wrote songs, not simply who *sang* them. Thus, they seemed an
entirely different sort of creative force on AM radio. For me,
the only thing comparable to them on black radio was a
singer named James Brown, who was an auteur; but Brown
seemed older to me, in many respects, so Brown's music did
not really speak to me as a young person, although it could
be said that his music spoke to me as a black person.

When "I'm a Loser" came out, I was in the eighth grade
and attending Bartlett Junior High School, an all-black

*James Miller, *Flowers in the Dustbin: The Rise of Rock and Roll, 1947–1977* (New York:
Simon & Schuster, 1999), p. 188.

school sandwiched between two housing projects, one on Thirteenth and Fitzwater streets and the other on Fifth and Carpenter. Each project was controlled by a street gang. Getting to and from school and surviving in the school was mostly a matter of trying to negotiate the spaces of these gangs. I did not learn much while I attended the school, but I was never bored, either, as I had to be constantly vigilant. For a time, my best friend there was a skinny, quiet Puerto Rican boy named Gilbert Perez. What we had in common was that we both listened to WIBG and we both loved the Beatles. Every day, at lunch or walking home from school together, we sang all the Beatles we knew: "Please Please Me," "I Feel Fine," "I'll Cry Instead," "Love Me Do," "Can't Buy Me Love," and "A Hard Day's Night." But the two we always sang, no matter what, were "I'm a Loser" and "Ticket to Ride." We even imitated the disc jockeys' intros to the songs. We were surely radio punks of the first order.

I do not think it ever quite occurred to us that we were two minority kids singing these "white" songs at a school where we were surely the only kids who knew or liked them. Our secret knowledge and secret sharing bonded us for that year as good friends but it did not especially estrange us from our "groups" or "categories." We did not think ourselves "disloyal" for liking the Beatles, nor did it make us identify as "white" or even with whites. We thought we were hip and enriched and that our love for the Beatles was helping us survive the school. We claimed the Beatles as our own music: the music of Gerald and Gilbert, and that was about it. We were the products of the zeitgeist of integration, and in our own way, we stitched together our fabric of a racially integrated life without actually interacting with white people for that year. I think we would have liked the Beatles less if we had had to share our appreciation of them with white fans in an integrated school. Today some might say we "appropriated" or culturally "expropriated" the Beatles in some reverse, "justified" fashion from the usual direction of racial "expropriation," and while that may have been true, such a formulation also misses the point because Gilbert and I were not acting ironically or self-consciously. We just thought it was good to like what you liked with someone else who liked it, too. Our liking the Beatles within the entire white pop context of WIBG, if it were to be seen as an act of resistance of some sort, was our innocent attempt to *not* be political or to have what we were doing be seen as political. We were, if anything, fighting, unknowingly, against the racial politicization of taste.

It might be thought that "I'm a Loser" appealed to us as adolescent boys unsure of ourselves in the world—in fact, feeling a bit of self-pity for liking the Beatles in the world that did not like them and did not appreciate our liking them—but that would not be true. The song, by John Lennon, about a boy who loses a girl he regrets losing and who tries to appear that he does not care, struck a deep chord with me emotionally at the time: I feared, as all adolescent boys do, of being a "loser," of being unattractive to girls (or to boys, I suppose, if you are gay), of being unattractive to yourself, of being someone who cannot get one's life together. The awk-

wardness of junior high underscores this fear, this tremendous insecurity, where the least little defect or miscue can be
ruinous—from wearing "jive," "homemade" clothes to eating
a Spam sandwich or getting government "surplus." But the
song was about a guy who hid the fact that he was a loser, so
it made me think in a more epistemological way: How do you
know if you are a loser? If you hide it or fake it well enough,
no one will know but you, and, if no one else knows, isn't that
the most important thing? In junior high, all I was trying to
do, with some reasonable success, was hide how much of a
loser I thought I was. My success at hiding it made me think
of myself as fairly clever and *not* a loser. Is life mostly about
hiding or faking one's most intimate realizations about one-
self? But if you cannot be real to other people, how can you
be real to yourself? Of course, this leads to the Pilate-like
question: What is real? When Lennon asks the question in
the song, if he cries for himself or for the girl, it was a powerful question about whether self-pity is entirely an act. Do we
act a certain way when we lose something because we think
that is the way we are supposed to act? How much do you
truly feel what you feel? The song mirrored the whole problem of the secret identity in superhero comics that Gilbert
and I so loved. Was Peter Parker more real when he was Peter
Parker or when he was Spider-Man? Was Clark Kent more
real when he was Superman? To adopt a line from the song:
We are not what we appear to be. To this day, this song hits a
deeper psychical chord with me than any other Beatles song.

    To be sure, the theme of the song is fairly standard fare in

American popular music, and there were two songs I knew at the time that were similar: Bobby Vee's "Take Good Care of My Baby" (1961), where the guy makes no attempt to disguise that he is a loser and hopes that he can make amends morally and practically by singing how much he wants the girl back if the new guy cannot make her happy, and Smokey Robinson and the Miracles' "The Tracks of My Tears" (1965), probably one of the most poetically sophisticated songs in the history of post–World War II American pop music, where the masquerade, elaborately dramatized in the lyrics, is entirely the point of the song. "I'm a Loser" is no match for the lyrical brilliance of "The Tracks of My Tears," but it is nonetheless a considerable accomplishment as a song, and what it expresses about the singer's situation is actually more complex than what's in the Robinson song because Lennon has a more detached point of view.

"I'm a Loser" was a sign of how Lennon and McCartney were beginning, during this period, to write more complex, challenging songs, largely because of the influence of Bob Dylan, to whom the Beatles had been listening since the end of 1963. As Lennon said about "I'm a Loser": "Instead of projecting myself into the situation, I would try to express what I felt about myself. I think it was Dylan who helped me realize that."* Barry Miles writes about the song: "The Dylan influence was obvious in other ways, too, from the acoustic

---

*Quoted in Barry Miles, *The Beatles Diary, Volume 1: The Beatles Years* (London: Omnibus Press, 2001), p. 179.

guitars powering the song to the use of the harmonica as a statement of passion."* The fact that Dylan met the Beatles in August 1964 and introduced them to marijuana also signaled the start of the Beatles' Dylan era. (It is a well-known story that Dylan thought "I Want to Hold Your Hand" was a song about drugs; he misheard the refrain as "I get high," instead of "I can't hide.")

I had heard almost no Dylan at the time of "I'm a Loser." But I had heard quite a lot of folk music, not only because of television shows like *Hootenanny* and the general popularity of folk at the time, with groups like Peter, Paul and Mary, and Trini Lopez's big hit version of Pete Seeger's "If I Had a Hammer," but also because my older sisters, who had become involved in the civil rights movement, started bringing home records with songs by Len Chandler, Bob Gibson, Phil Ochs, and Buffy Sainte-Marie. "I'm a Loser" felt a lot like some of those songs, and those songs had the romance of youth and the energy of protest behind them. It was the lyrical restlessness and yearning in this music that I found intoxicating, and that is why I liked "I'm a Loser" so much.

I went to a different school in the ninth grade and never saw Gilbert Perez again. The Beatles would also fall away from me for a time, and I would not pick them up again on AM radio until "Hey Jude." But that is another story.

But in walking home from school every day past the neighborhood State Store (the only store authorized to sell

*Miles, *The Beatles Diary, Volume 1: The Beatles Years*, p. 179.

liquor in Pennsylvania), I realized implicitly another meaning for the Beatles' song. In some larger sense, "I'm a Loser"
was a cautionary song for me, a warning about what could
happen to me if I did not go to another school and did not
try to get another life apart from the neighborhood in which
I grew up. After the eighth grade, I was never to feel much
attachment to my neighborhood again. I had not grown up
by any means, but I had outgrown what the neighborhood
could offer me under the racial and political circumstances
of my youth. I had seen more than enough of self-pity in
many of the black men in my neighborhood: disfigured,
alcoholic, unemployed, directionless, sometimes senselessly
violent, sometimes preyed upon by violence, trapped in a
kind of social-welfare nightmare that was particularly shameful in the accusing eyes of the neighborhood's whites.

And these men would be gathered around the State Store,
sharing a bottle, cadging money to buy a bottle. And the only
seeming escape from self-pity that these men could offer me
was an anger so destructive that it was bound to kill its pos-
sessors and everything around them, including what was
worth saving. I would walk past these men every day and say
to myself, "I'm no loser! I'm no loser!" Some kids could joke
about these men and their lives with such cynical aplomb that
I was slowly convinced that it took too much to laugh. And
crying would do me no good. I needed an exit. The year that I
discovered and sang "I'm a Loser," which told me "Beware
self-pity," was when, in my childhood, everything changed.

YeSTeRDay

PICO IYER

I'M SITTING IN A LOVE HOTEL in Osaka, with Hiroko, the unreasonably glamorous, bright-eyed, passionate young woman from Kyoto who's become my love. The toilet seat in the pink bathroom has as many controls as the 747 I'm about to board, and there are more buttons and dials around the bed than in the airport nearby. Love hotels are as wildly imaginative and stylish in impeccably segregated Japan as regular hotels are by-the-book and flairless; this is the realm of play, the country has determined, which means that all these places called Prestige and Charme and New Seeds are as far from the domestic realm as the red-lit lanterns of the "entertainment quarter" are from the fluorescent, Western-style bulbs that expose us all at home.

But *play* in this instance means pushing a button to acti-vate a song on the karaoke screen before us, and this has left me in a tricky situation. As a lifelong traveler, I've grown to be an expert in turning tail, in looking in two directions at once. When it comes to songs, I'm far too likely to take *simplicity* to be a pretty word for ignorance.

Three hours from now, I'll be flying away again. And I've taken pains never to share with Hiroko some of my favorite ballads—"Late for the Sky," "Call It a Loan," "My Opening Farewell"—because, once translated, they'll bring home to her that all of them are about flights, in every ambiguous sense of that word. They're complex love songs that are perhaps too dear to a would-be writer's heart; they turn—as in a tangle of twisted sheets at dawn—on all the convulsions and gyrations of love: the rueful aftereffects, the mixed feelings, the frustrated helplessness before one's own un-helpful needs.

A transparent love song seems silly to me, the stuff of adolescence; perhaps I've grown too attached to things that turn in opposite directions—the child's version of maturity—and to double-sidedness as something that will give my imagination the most to play with.

Trains every day, leaving either way; telling you when I came I was a stranger; running for that morning light, through the whispered promises and the changing light: our poets have always been expert at giving beautiful expression to their treacheries and the ways they prefer their blank pages to the fullness of real life. And I've grown very drawn to those whose first loyalty is to the desk.

Besides, I tell myself, an enchanted foreigner, Japan—and Hiroko's birthplace of Kyoto in particular—is the spiritual home of the "morning-after poem"; in the tenth-century

Heian culture that has drawn me here, part of the point of spending a night together is to commemorate the fleeting moment in a few lines that might prove a little less fleeting than the predawn good-bye.

Experience can never be as pretty as the artful package we make of it.

HIROKO IS AS MUCH AT A LOSS amid all the high-tech gizmos in the room as I am, though one way in which she confounds me is by being so full-throated a mix of absolute innocence and surrender. I've never met a woman who gives herself so completely to emotion, even as she is as capable and practical as the vending machines from which she so deftly draws her cans of hot café au lait. Hand yourself entirely over to dream, her culture might be telling us—so long as you never begin to confuse it with reality.

Several times a day she changes, from black leather jacket to picture-perfect headband and leggings for the health club, to slinky black dress and even teddy-bear pajamas, while I look on in my unwashed clothes and don't know whether I'm watching a performance or (more likely) an entirely sincere and wholehearted possession of a part.

Play yourself as if it were real, Japan says; you can and should be earnest and candid in the performance of all your contradictory parts. We all do this, showing one face to our mothers and another to our bosses; the only hypocrisy is to pretend it isn't the case.

She narrows her eyes and her silky waterfall of dark hair tickles me as she rises.

IN ONE CORNER of the room is a television, though this one comes with a microphone. This is the instrument with which Hiroko seems most comfortable, if only because going to karaoke bars—performing passion professionally in the most public of spaces—is as much a part of Japanese life as are privacy, intimacy, and silence.

A sentence comes up on-screen and she hands me the mike. We have only three hours in the room, chosen from a panel of illuminated screens outside the curtained entrance of the place; we never see the person at the kiosk into which we've slipped the equivalent of two twenties in cash. Unsure what to do with the high-end colognes by the sink or the nozzles in the shower, we seem to have decided that this is the way we can make the most of our brief stay in a parallel world.

"Your choice," she says.

Hiroko has an angel's voice, high and faultless, with which she often sings me lullabies. Songs about thunder and spirits, though they're all really about putting us at peace. There's plenty of anguish in the melancholy folk ditties she delivers, but anguish is meant to be sweeter than pleasure in Japan, so long as it can be relished from a safe distance.

We've been together long enough by now—three years— for her to know I can't carry a tune. And for me to know that she wouldn't make a request that stood any chance of being refused.

"You first," I say.

"No. Please."

Her eyes are alight, imploring; she knows how to forget, for three hours, that by this evening I'll be on my way to a far side of the world.

I think of the simplest song I know.

Of course, it's also the song that all Japanese count on foreigners delivering when suddenly handed a microphone; it's the one that's very hard to get wrong—as simple as a lullaby, really—and its words go through my head as an advertising jingle might. Or, in fact, as the hymns I had to sing at school that I remember as I don't any of the poems I was made to learn.

Somehow, on this one outing, Paul McCartney wrote words that go into you without your knowing it, until they come out at the other end—accompanied by a melody as second nature as "Greensleeves." Later I will learn that the lyrics came to him on a drive from the airport in southeastern Portugal and the tune appeared so magically in his head one morning that he assumed he must have "pinched" it, replaying a series of notes he'd heard somewhere else.

At some point, I'll hear that he even managed to sing the lyrics "scrambled eggs" to what seemed to him a tune he must have borrowed. But still, how can I resist a song that's barely two minutes long and about a game to play and the wish to hide away?

"Yesterday . . ." I begin to say (or "sing"), in part so we won't think of tomorrow. The tune is perfect for Japan: all the silvery beauty, the mournfulness of autumn. The beauty that comes as the daughter of things ending; the sentiment cherished precisely because it's disappearing around a corner.

The self-pity, too, of the man left behind, hurt and bewildered; the only thing he has to believe in, the yesterday that at some level doesn't exist.

It is a theory I will develop in later years that the artists I don't love are often capable of songs I'll always cherish if they're simple to the point of being everyone's, generic. "Kathy's Song" by Paul Simon; "As Tears Go By," which even the Stones often proclaim as embarrassing; "Fields of Gold" by Sting, the singer I have pledged to hate, if only because Hiroko and every other woman seem to love him.

Van Morrison, Leonard Cohen, Joni Mitchell; the heroes I cherish would seldom commit themselves to songs as bare and transparent as these. Van repeats nonsense syllables, again and again, enclosed in his own trance, till we're beyond the realm of words altogether and feeling the sensations of an Albion of the mind we don't begin to need to understand; Leonard turns over the self-betraying cruelties of the heart with a density and grave sophistication that owe as much to Donne and the Metaphysicals as to the Hank Williams he celebrates. And there'll never be a song so plangent and devastating as "A Case of You," devoted to that very elusiveness in Cohen, and how much of him comes out in a woman he's loved, whether he—or she—wants it or not.

But the Beatles have never been a group I've enjoyed. Lennon comes off as too cynical, the sardonic voice of an England I've spent my life trying to put behind me, while Paul sometimes seems the irresistible counter-John who tries to appease those of us hungry for more sweetness.

Ringo fits the part that the country now plays in the global imagination—droll, madcap jester to the world—and George's heart might have been in the right place, but I'd put good money on the fact that he left his mind in San Francisco, or on the way to some ashram in Rishikesh.

The Beatles for me have a rare gift for being too simple or too sophisticated, too worldly or too much the opposite, and I am (almost defiantly) immune to their charms. I never mourned their breakup, and I never revisit their tunes.

But McCartney's account of a desertion has the timelessness of a folk ballad sung by a man from no particular culture or age, and attributed to "Anonymous." It's everybody's song (like "Your Song," another example of how piercing and lovely can be a straight-ahead love song from a singer I would gladly pay never to listen to again). It hardly matters that, decades on, the writer of the world's favorite ballad will realize it's about a mother, not a girl.

To anyone who loves the Beatles, the song may well be an embarrassment. The first song he'd like to repudiate, the elevator music that betrays everything the boyish revolutionaries are famous for. The most popular song in the world this side of "Happy Birthday," it's said, which will come to seem even more saccharine and flimsy because, like "Hallelujah," like "One," it's repeated almost every time a karaoke singer picks up a mike.

But Hiroko is looking up at me, and our 180 minutes are ticking away. The plane that's due to carry me off to the New World will be landing soon, and before the day is out we'll be at the security checkpoint, and I'll be feeling doubly bad that the words of the song don't apply to me at all. Most of our discussions are implicitly about yesterday and tomorrow: what my plans are for our lives, whether we ought to be pledged to a New World that is always looking to the future, or to weighted Japan, in which lives are defined by what has already happened through nine hundred thousand yesterdays.

It's the simplest, shortest song I know, and even if sung badly, it will have the charm and undefended openness of a nursery rhyme. It is the country-and-western lament we Beatles haters cling to, if only because it seems to suggest how thin the group's talent is. It's an open confession that makes you see how the one rejected in love inspired love in the first place.

THIS WAS ALL MORE THAN a quarter century ago, and Hiroko and I have been married now for decades. I've edged much closer, over the years, to a sense that tomorrow is seldom wiser than yesterday, any more than young America is a useful mentor for seasoned Japan. Hiroko now takes flights everywhere, by my side. She doesn't have to look at me through tears as I walk through the security check, ready to strap myself into a new identity. We don't need karaoke screens, because we spend the hours before a flight at home.

Yet I'll never forget wanting to thank "Yesterday" for getting me off the hook in a difficult situation and for helping us pretend that love was easy as regret and that things were simple, sweet.

Had I chosen "So Long, Marianne" or "Hey, That's No Way to Say Goodbye," had I looked for something Shakespearean in its doubleness, God only knows (that's another one, courtesy of Brian Wilson) how long "Yesterday" might be playing in my head, a fact of life as much as a song on-screen infuriatingly impossible to forget. Had I not chosen a pretty ditty that Hiroko could take in as readily as the child's ballad it resembles, I might even now be alone, with a worn copy of Elvis Costello's greatest love songs in my hands. All Hiroko was trying to do, I understand now, was what both Japan and Paul McCartney manage so effortlessly: to ease me into a simplicity that fool writers are tempted to refute.

NORWEGIAN WOOD

AMY BLOOM

I WATCHED THE BEATLES for the first time from a copper-colored shag rug in our basement, also our TV room, on February 9, 1964. My father sat behind me in his recliner, smoking a cigar and shaking his head. My father had been shaking his head (I gathered) for the last fifteen years. He liked show tunes. He liked Gilbert and Sullivan (he could sing *The Pirates of Penzance* in Yiddish) and he liked Peggy Lee. He thought Sinatra was an asshole, Elvis was ridiculous, and the Beatles were the kind of thing, like puppies, like cotton candy, that young girls would like.

I sat as close to the screen as my parents would allow. This was 1964, so that was very close. My nose was five inches away from the screen. The Beatles came out in their silly suits. They shook their heads and their glossy hair undulated like satin. Even Ringo, who was worse than plain (back then), had nice hair. They sang "All My Loving," and girls in the audience screamed as if they were being tossed off cliffs. They sang "She Loves You," and I watched girls in the audience faint. My father chortled. I flopped around on the floor, like a seal. In the second half of the show, the Beatles crescendoed with "I Want to Hold Your Hand," and it looked like girls in the audience were actually dying. I banged my hands and feet on the linoleum, because I couldn't contain myself. My father said, "Calm down," and then there were other acts. Frank Gorshin did an impersonation of Kirk Douglas or Burt Lancaster and I crawled onto the couch, to calm down.

A year later, I was twelve. I knew what I knew. Ethan R. had led me to his bedroom while our mothers had coffee in the kitchen. He unbuttoned my shirt. (He was thirteen.) He admired my pink and new bra. We lay on his bed, holding hands and staring at the ceiling. We agreed that we really, really liked the Beatles. He said George was the real talent of the group. He played "Norwegian Wood" twice on his record player, singing along, and the third time he got up to move the needle back to the beginning, I grabbed my sneakers and ran downstairs. I was not doing any fooling around with someone who sang along. Who liked the dopiest song on the album. Whose favorite Beatle was George.

My sixth-grade spring was slow. I had nothing else to do, so I listened to the Beatles every afternoon, and I decided that somehow Ethan, in not running after me, had jilted me. I became, a little abruptly, lovesick. My mother called his mother, who told my mother that we hadn't seen or spoken to each other since February. I played "I'm Looking Through You" a hundred times. I went about my sixth-grade business, muttering darkly in the library, and during kickball, "Love has a nasty habit of disappearing overnight . . ." I wore my big sister's black turtleneck. (Alas, I was still wearing saddle shoes.)

Happily, my parents sent me to sleepaway camp, where everyone, all the counselors and campers, were listening to the Beatles. My bunk counselor also listened to Joan Baez in private, when she could, but when she wanted us to pull ourselves together, and stop torturing the scapegoat or trying on mascara or climbing onto the roof of the boys' cabin and dropping water balloons, she let us listen to *Rubber Soul*.

There was a dance. I wore pink madras Bermuda shorts and a pink pleather headband and a white blouse with a Peter Pan collar to the dance. I had begged my mother for pink loafers, which I wore, with Hepburn-like élan, without socks. It paid off. A boy who was taller than me, who did not wear glasses, who did not have acne, asked me to dance. Richard could dance. Ethan was dead to me. We did the Twist and the Hully Gully. We Hitchhiked and Monkeyed and Frugged. He was unstoppable, and whenever we got separated on the dance floor, he would pop up with a wave and a new move. At some point, I lost my headband. I had a boyfriend.

We listened to the Beatles for the next two weeks. We held hands where Uncle Howie, the camp's owner, couldn't see us. We blinked twice when we passed each other in the dining hall. We volunteered to put out the camp newspaper, and Richard brought his transistor radio, and there were, reliably, hours of Beatles and awkward kissing. (He did wear glasses, after all. His best friend had told him not to wear them to the dance. We would fold his horn-rims and my pink harlequins side by side and squeeze into the ancient corduroy armchair near the mimeo machine.) Camp ended. We went to different junior highs. My sister told me I couldn't call him, so I didn't. A friend of mine said she had seen him in Scotto's Pizza with another girl. An eighth-grader. I knew. I listened to "In My Life" and wept to every tragic, elegiac line of it.

I covered my room with posters of Allen Ginsberg and Jimi Hendrix. The Chambers Brothers were over my bed. I worshipped Aretha Franklin, Nina Simone, and Ernestine Anderson. I did listen to *Revolver* and *Sgt. Pepper* and *Magical Mystery Tour* and even the White Album in 1968, because you couldn't be the kind of girl I was and not, but I had moved on and I didn't care.

Ask me today, and I can sing every line of every song on *Rubber Soul* and remember every moment of my heart beating fast, and the sweaty palms and that particularly sweet heartbreak, mostly real, a little synthetic and sweet, because, even crying in my bed, I knew it'd pass. When I was fifteen, I understood that the Beatles represented innocence, and for what was coming next, they couldn't help me.

ELEANOR RIGBY

REBECCA MEAD

WHEN MY FRIEND CHRISSIE told me that her dad had installed a mobile home outside the back of her house, across the street from mine, I was envious at first. We were young—eight? nine?—I don't remember exactly, but we were young enough, anyway, for this to seem like a piece of outrageously good fortune. The mobile home—what we in the England of my childhood called a caravan—appeared one day behind Chrissie's garage, parked on the concrete path that lead from the kitchen door to the yard. It felt as if it had materialized just for us to play in: a scaled-down house on wheels, with upholstered benches that transformed into narrow beds, a Formica table that folded down, a tiny kitchen, and frilly curtains on the windows, just like those from behind which the residents on our street could spy upon the goings-on of their neighbors.

On the first few days that the caravan was there, we had the run of it. It was summer, and the interior was stuffy. It must have been bought secondhand, and had an already lived-in atmosphere. That was fine with us, since we imagined that we were the people who had already lived in it: gypsies on the road, or runaways who had joined the circus. Chrissie's parents had their house, a three-bedroom, semidetached home, built in the 1950s. Chrissie's bedroom was the mirror image of my own bedroom across the street. Now we had *our* house. What other possible function could the caravan serve than to be a stage for children's fantasy play?

Somehow, though, we learned that, henceforth, the caravan would be off-limits. Chrissie's dad was moving out of the house and into it. What this would mean for Chrissie was beyond my comprehension, or even concern. I focused on the caravan. Why would someone's dad move into the backyard? Weren't dads supposed to live with their families? That was the end of my envy of Chrissie, and the beginning of something new: a sense of the unsettling mysteries of adult lives.

I CAN'T EXPLAIN EXACTLY how or why "Eleanor Rigby" became linked in my mind with Chrissie's family—with the caravan in the garden, and her father's decampment, and the unraveling of the marriage that followed, and Chrissie's dad moving to a flat a half mile away, and Chrissie's mum moving to a small terraced house, and Chrissie and her older sister, Catherine, having a complicated divided life instead of a simple, unified one. (I've changed their names.) It would make for a neater narrative to say I heard the record played at

Chrissie's house, or listened to it on the car radio as her mother drove us to Brownies. It would be a better story if I could write that I remember it being the song that Chrissie's mother would play over and over again, gin and tonic in hand, as she sat at the dining room table in her solitary evenings and looked through rain-streaked windows at the yellow-lit windows of the caravan; or that it was Chrissie's father's favorite disc, the one he balanced on the spindle of the portable record player he installed in his backyard retreat, the staccato volley of orchestral strings in a minor key emanating from behind the caravan's poorly insulated panes.

But all those scenarios are invented. There's no such straightforward connection between the song and that period of my life. The link is more associative. I'm aware of a wispy, ungraspable set of emotions—the kind of half-rational, half-fantastical linkages that psychoanalysts tease out of dream imagery. All I know for sure is that whenever I hear the bowing of those violins—the string octet was arranged by George Martin, and the microphone was placed close to the strings, so as to give an intimacy of sound that was unprecedented—it brings me back to that transitional period in my childhood when I began to discern that the adults I knew had hidden dimensions to their lives. In its melancholy, suggestive imagery, and its urgent, desolate melody, "Eleanor Rigby" reminds me of when I first learned that adults might have roles other than those in which I had unimaginatively cast them—that of providing the untroubled backdrop to the dramas of children.

Until Chrissie's father moved into the backyard it had been the children's domain—as were all the back gardens of the kids in our neighborhood. We lived on a quiet, little-trafficked road in our provincial seaside English town, and we were in and out of one another's houses from an early age, without intrusive oversight from our mothers, most of whom didn't have jobs, or our fathers, most of whom did. At my house, there was a swing set in the garden. Next door, at the foot of Claire's garden, there was a musty, cobweb-filled, corrugated-iron shelter left over from World War II, which a group of us converted into a clubhouse, requiring secret passwords to enter. When Chrissie's sister, Catherine, was smaller, Chrissie's dad had installed a jungle gym at the end of their garden. Catherine was too old to play with us now: she was on the cusp of adolescence, already in secondary school, interested in makeup and boys. The wooden seats on the seesaw had started to rot, and the slide was battered.

But Chrissie and I spent hours playing there, clambering on steel bars that were cold to our hands, inventing compli-cated dramatic scenarios that we would act out—stories of adventure and escape, in which we were friends at the mercy of dangerous forces. Sometimes we set off on foot to explore what was known as the moor, an uncultivated sprawl of land and backwater marsh between our street and the beach, about a mile away. We were free to roam unsupervised along its rush-edged paths through boggy swamps, since nobody had yet started to fear the harm that unfamiliar adults might do to children. The incidental damage that familiar adults—fathers, mothers—might do to their children while living their own lives, well, that was another matter.

LIKE MANY PEOPLE of my generation, I never "discovered" the Beatles: they were always already there. I was born in 1966, seven weeks after "Eleanor Rigby" was released as a single and spent a month at the top of the British charts. I arrived into a world in which the Beatles were, as John Lennon had pointed out a few months earlier, "more popular than Jesus."

I grew up hearing them: their early jangling guitar-driven love songs and their late hypnotic experiments were simply part of the atmosphere. But I didn't grow up listening to them. My parents weren't Beatles aficionados. There were no Beatles discs in their limited record collection. By the standards of the sixties, my mother and father came to parenthood late: my mother was thirty-five when I was born, far older than most of the other mothers in the playgrounds of Putney, the area of London in which we lived for the first three years of my life, before moving to a seaside town on the south coast. My mother and father had come of age listening to the music that came before the Beatles—the music that the Beatles surpassed and swept away. Frank Sinatra's *Songs for Swingin' Lovers*, released ten years before I was born, was the soundtrack of their youth, and the first song lyrics I ever absorbed without trying were those to "You Make Me Feel So Young," which my parents would sing while waltzing me, or my older brother, or sometimes each other, around the living room.

If they were too old for the Beatles, I was too young. I was only three when the band broke up, and so they were gone before I could have known they'd been there. I didn't start to come to musical consciousness until the late seventies, just in time to witness the Clash and the Sex Pistols emerging to enact their own gestures of generational revolution. My own coming-of-age album was *Never Mind the Bollocks*, released in 1977. To the extent that I was aware of knowing anything about the Beatles at that time, I knew them as the band Paul McCartney had been in before he started wandering through the Scottish Highlands in knee-high boots and cascading curls, strumming a guitar and singing "Mull of Kintyre" to the accompanying swirl of parading bagpipers. That didn't seem to be the highest recommendation.

I didn't know then that McCartney was the principal author of "Eleanor Rigby." I might have shown Wings more respect if I had. If "Mull of Kintyre" is a pub-at-closing-time ditty—McCartney at his most sentimental and fatally catchy—"Eleanor Rigby" is a perfectly constructed and controlled narrative. It eschews the usual preoccupations of pop songs, including many of the pop songs that made the Beatles famous. It is not about young love, especially not about youthful sexual desire, and the lead vocalist is not the song's subject. The song does not announce, "I love you," or any of the infinite variations thereupon to which popular songwriters inveterately turn.

There is, indeed, no "I" and "you" in "Eleanor Rigby." It's the first pop song I consciously recognized as being neither a confession nor an incitement, but something quite different: a work of fiction. The complex subjectivities of its two protagonists are barely revealed, but resonantly implied. It's a song, but it's also a short story—one that is as puzzling and suggestive as the actions of an unhappily married father who moves into a home outside the home.

"I've just got to put my face on," my mother would say when she was getting ready to go out of our house, applying foundation, lipstick, mascara. I grew up thinking that there was nothing odd about a woman's face being found in a jar, and it made sense that Eleanor Rigby's was, too. It was not a mask to hide behind, but an appearance to keep up—a way of being presentable in the world, at least if one was a woman over the age of forty.

I remember the face that Chrissie's mom wore when she was out in public: green eyeliner, black lashes, and bright lipstick that was set off by her dark hair, which she wore in curls cut close to her head. Her clothes, too, were bold: bright patterns and rich colors. She had a full-time job, which set her apart from the other mothers and made her mysterious. There was an edge of theatricality to her demeanor, and a frankness that sometimes surprised me. "You'll be a good-looking woman when you grow up," she once told me, with a note of reassurance in her voice, and it's a remark I have never forgotten. This is not just because of what it painfully implied about my not-yet-grown-up appearance—I was thin, dark, small, not pretty like Chrissie, who was fair and blue-eyed. It is also because it gave me a way to look forward to a future in which things might be different for me—to a future when I would be old enough to have acquired my own jars of makeup, and whatever kind of life went with them. It gave me a sense of the advantages that might accompany maturity, but also an idea of the vulnerability that came with being a grown-up rather than a girl.

THERE WAS NO REAL Eleanor Rigby, although for years, Beatles fans have frequented a grave belonging to a woman of that name, who died in 1944 and was buried in the grave-yard of St. Peter's Church, Woolton, Liverpool. Strangely enough, this is the church in the hall of which the young Paul McCartney and John Lennon had their first encounter, and biographers have suggested that the name, glimpsed on a tombstone, may have lodged in McCartney's mind only to reemerge later, artistically reconfigured.

This Eleanor Rigby died young—she was only forty-four—and childless. But she was married: the tombstone de-scribes her as the wife of Thomas Woods. This peculiarity of nomenclature is the kind of thing that might register with an observant and thoughtful young person passing through the graveyard. Wives did not keep their maiden names, nei-ther in the time of McCartney's childhood, nor in my own. I only ever knew Chrissie's mom to have Chrissie's dad's last name, even after the arrival of the caravan, and the separa-

tion, and the divorce. A woman's name was the first possession she surrendered in marriage; and yet the real-life Eleanor
Rigby seems to have kept hers, at least in death.

In 1966, McCartney told an interviewer, Hunter Davies,
that the lyrics for the song came "out of our imagination,"
as did all of their songs. McCartney first came up with the
tune sitting at the piano, playing to himself. The name Eleanor Rigby was a later inspiration: in his first, sketchy attempt, the lonely woman at the center of the song had been
called Sadie Hawkins. The next day, he'd decided to include
a priest, Father McCartney, but hadn't yet decided what to
do with him.

It was not until McCartney went to John Lennon's house
and played the song to his bandmates and some other friends
that the rest of it fell into place. Paul did not want the song to
appear to be about a relative, and so someone found McKenzie
in the phone book as a replacement for McCartney. Ringo
Starr came up with the utterly apt prosaic activity for the solitary priest: darning his clerical hosiery, an activity that a man
sworn to celibacy would be obliged to do for himself. George
Harrison contributed the repeated refrain. From that afternoon's conversation came the idea that crystallizes and com-
pletes the song's genius, in its third and final verse. These two
isolated individuals *are* ultimately united, but only through
the agency of death, which brings them together in the church
and churchyard. This song, which so perfectly captures the
pathos of loneliness, was generated in an atmosphere of intimacy and friendship. It was a product of the extraordinarily

fruitful four-way marriage that was the Beatles collaboration, until that marriage ended.

AFTER CHRISSIE MOVED AWAY with her mum we still saw
each other, even though we could no longer run across the
street to each other's houses. But at eleven, we were assigned
to different schools, and our lives diverged in other ways,
too. My older brother was readying himself to leave for
university. Chrissie's older sister had a baby in her late teens.
Chrissie became an aunt, familiar with the changing of dia-
pers and the sterilizing of bottles before she had really left
childhood herself. When I visited her house, which was increasingly infrequently, it was cluttered with brightly colored toys, and there was an unfamiliar sour-sweet smell in
the air.

Within a few weeks of writing and recording "Eleanor
Rigby," McCartney conceived of a very different song that
would end up being the opposite side of that single's release:
"Yellow Submarine." If there is any Beatles tune that I remember being deliberately played during my childhood, this
is it: a nonsense song with musical-hall rhythms and surreal-
ist lyrics, a track that parents would play during freeze-dance
games at birthday parties, and kids would sing along to. Giving an account of its inspiration, McCartney said that he was
inspired by the imaginations of children, and wanted to write
a song specifically to appeal to them: a tune to go with the

bright plastic rattles and blocks that now had been handed down from Chrissie to Chrissie's niece.

I've always loathed "Yellow Submarine." As a child, I found it confusing, and I disliked being confused by it. Even as the song seemed to issue an invitation into a world of carefree liberty—living forever in a yellow submarine with all of one's friends—I sensed a more dangerous subtext.

"Yellow Submarine" describes a world without responsibility, an impossible bubble in which the games go on forever. On the flip side of that nonsense is the gravity offered by "Eleanor Rigby," with its depiction of lonely lives in which isolation is not a childish joy but a sober adult reality. Sparsely but vividly, "Eleanor Rigby" conjures a truth I first discerned when I learned that a caravan—no less than a yellow submarine—might be something other than a vehicle for escapism, something more than a place in which to play. It might equally serve as a metaphorical conveyance to a world in which innocence is no longer an option—a world in which the mysterious, half-glimpsed-at stories of Eleanor Rigby and Father McKenzie offer their own, utterly intelligible truth.

YELLOW SUBMARINE

MARIA POPOVA

MY PARENTS FELL IN LOVE on a train. It was the middle of the Cold War and they were both traveling from their native Bulgaria to Saint Petersburg in Russia, where they were to attend different universities—my father, an introvert of formidable intelligence, was studying computer science; my mother, a poetry-writing (bordering-on-bossy) extrovert, library science.

An otherwise rational man, my father describes the train encounter as love at first sight. Upon arrival, he began courting my mother with such subtlety that it took her two years to realize she was being courted.

One spring morning, having finally begun to feel like a couple, they were walking across the lawn between the two dorms and decided it was time for them to have a whistle-call. At the time, Bulgarian couples customarily had whistle-calls—distinctive tunes they came up with, usually borrowed from the melody of a favorite song, by which they could find each other in a crowd or summon each other from across the street.

Partway between the primitive and the poetic, between the mating calls of mammals and the sonnets by which Romeo and Juliet beckoned each other, these signals were part of a couple's shared language, a private code to be performed in public. Both sets of my grandparents had one. My mother's parents, elementary school teachers in rural Bulgaria who tended to an orchard and the occasional farm animal, used a melody of unclear origin but aurally evocative of a Bulgarian folk song; my father's parents, both civil engineers and city intellectuals, used a fragment from a Schumann waltz.

THAT SPRING MORNING, knowing that my mother was a Beatles fan, my father suggested "Yellow Submarine." There was no deliberation, no getting mired in the paradox of choice—just an instinctive offering fetched from some mysterious mental library.

Eventually, my parents got pregnant, got married, had this child. They continued to summon each other, and eventually me, by whistling "Yellow Submarine." Although I didn't know at the time that it was originally written as a children's song, it came to color my childhood. I had always wondered why, of all possible songs saturating their youth, my parents had chosen "Yellow Submarine"—a song released long before they met. My father wasn't much of a Beatles fan himself, and yet that spring morning he was able to open the cabinet of his semiconscious memory, fetch a melody he had heard almost twenty years earlier, and effortlessly whistle it to his beloved. The familial whistle-call became a given in my childhood, like math homework and beef Stroganoff Sundays, so it wasn't until I was in my early thirties that it occurred to me to inquire about how "Yellow Submarine" wove itself into the family fabric. The story of how that seemingly random song had implanted itself in my father's mind is the archetypal story of how popular music, and perhaps all popular art, is metabolized in the body of culture. Once it has entered the crucible of consciousness, a song becomes subject to a peculiar alchemy—the particularities of the listener's life at that particular moment transmute its objective meaning, if there ever was one at all, into a subjective impression. That impression is what we encode into memory, what we retrieve to whistle twenty years later. The artist's original intent is melded with the listener's personal context into an amorphous mass of inexpressible yet unforgettable unity—a dormant seed whose blossoming depends on the myriad factors fertilizing the surrounding soil. That the seed was planted at all may remain unheralded until the moment of its blossoming.

My great-grandfather—my father's maternal grandfather—was an astronomer and mathematician born at the dawn of the twentieth century into Bulgaria's nascent monarchy, which followed five hundred years of Ottoman slavery. He lived through two world wars, then watched his homeland, battered by centuries of oppression and brutalized by decades of war, crumble into communism when the monarchy was overthrown in the 1940s. The pernicious anti-intellectualism of the communist regime took great pains to silence any cultural signal from the other side of the Iron Curtain. On the radio—then the dominant form of mass media—Western broadcasts in translation were banned and their frequencies muffled. But because so few Bulgarians spoke non-Slavic languages, the government didn't bother to muffle foreign broadcasts in the original—those were just buried on hard-to-find frequencies.

Witnessing the timorous promise of freedom succumb to dictatorship must have been unbearable for my great-grandfather. Somehow, he hacked his transistor radio into the frequency of the BBC World Service and, well into his fifties by that point, set about teaching himself English. He acquired an English dictionary and a few literary classics through some underground channel—from Jane Austen to first-edition Hemingways, which survive to this day in my grandmother's library—and began underlining words, filling the margins with translations, and code-cracking English grammar. It was a small act of rebellion, but a monumental one. By the 1960s, he had become fluent in English, with the BBC as his sole conduit to the other side—a lifeline of intellectual liberty.

When his nine grandchildren were entrusted in his day-time care, he decided to weave this surreptitious insurgency into his legacy by teaching them English. He would take them to the park, and when the time came for their afternoon snack, he wouldn't feed them until they were able to ask for their sandwiches in proper Queen's English.

The BBC World Service was always on in the kitchen, and in the late summer of 1966, just before my father's sixth birthday, "Yellow Submarine" was on heavy rotation—it had been released on August 5. One morning, my great-grandfather decided to use the song as an opportunity for another English lesson with the kids. Perhaps because this was in Varna—Bulgaria's naval capital, where the city's celebrated Naval Museum is still housed in a giant decommissioned submarine—and perhaps simply because he was a little boy and little boys have such obsessions, my father was enamored of submarines and instantly took the bait. He fell in love with the song, learned its melody, and memorized the lyrics.

He grew up fluent in English and German (my great-grandfather had also hacked his way into the Deutsche Welle), and although his obsession with the engineering of military vehicles and vessels never left him, the yellow submarine became a distant childhood memory. But it left a vestige, invisible and dormant until it was fertilized by the unlikeliest—or is it the likeliest?—of catalysts: love. The garden of life is strewn with such dormant seeds and so much of art blossoms from their unwilled and unwillable awakenings. In a marvelous yet hardly surprising parallel, the very origin of "Yellow Submarine" intimates such boyhood vestiges.

Paul McCartney wrote the song as a nonsense children's rhyme to which the Beatles added an irreverent edge.

In the town where I was born
Lived a man who sailed to sea

McCartney's grandfather, Joseph, grew up near the Liverpool docks and played the E-flat bass, a giant tuba-like brass instrument. Lennon's grandfather, George, was a lifelong mariner who was aboard one of the first three-masted ships to sail around the world. After he met his wife at the bustling old Roman seaport of Chester, he retired into domesticity by taking a shoreside job recovering wreckage from sunk submarines. McCartney later recounted that he wrote "Yellow Submarine" by making up a melody in his head and letting it carry the story of "an ancient mariner, telling the young kids where he'd lived." Could this "man who sailed the sea" be an amalgam of these two boyhood vestiges?

It is, of course, a perennial mystery how the innumerable fragments of experience we amass in the course of living come into contact with one another, how they are fused together in the combinatorial process of creativity and transformed into something new. Impatient with mystery, we tend to seek to fill the unknown with easy explanations. When "Yellow Submarine" was released—on the other side of "Eleanor Rigby," on the same day as *Revolver*—people rushed to presumptions about the obvious agent of transmutation. This, after all, was the middle of the 1960s and the Beatles had just begun experimenting with psychedelics. But while John and George were busting open the doors of perception with acid, Paul was largely uninterested in such synthetic aids—bursting with creative energy, his spiritual electricity was self-synthesized. Although he insisted over and over on the innocuous origin of the song, throngs of critics both professional and self-appointed continued to interpret the song as an ode to psychedelics.

If psychedelics played a role at all, it was indirect—at most as a cross-pollinating agent of adjacent imaginations. Since the Beatles shared so much of their lives, Paul was inevitably immersed in his bandmates' newfound wonderland of psychedelia and absorbed its rousing visual language. According to a Beatles intimate quoted in Bob Spitz's excellent biography of the Fab Four, one of those early acid experiences produced "marvelous visions" of "rainbow-colored submarines"—an image so wild and whimsical that John and George, in their wide-eyed exhilaration, likely enthused about it to the rest. Paul might have folded that image into his mental catalog of fragments—in fact, his first draft of the lyrics included multiple submarines of various colors before they were distilled into the sole yellow submarine. (Donovan added the blue sky and green sea—a welcome reinjection of color into the final yellow monochrome.)

McCartney had written the song for Ringo Starr, who was "very good with kids," deliberately keeping it "not too rangey in the vocal range" for Ringo to perform. It was a perfect fit—the song became by far the most successful Beatles track with Ringo as a vocalist. But there was something else, something singularly magical, that lent it timeless luster and increasingly timely allure today. Its recording was a jubilant celebration of phenomena that have since gone just about extinct—the communal element of making art and the messy, hands-on craftsmanship of sound.

On May 26, 1966, the Beatles packed into Studio Two along with a motley cast of Abbey Road regulars and irregulars, spearheaded by legendary producer George Martin.

And our friends are all on board

The gang proceeded to fetch an arsenal of noisemaking tools from the utility closet—chains, whistles, buckets, glasses, wind makers, thunderstorm machines, wartime hand bells, hooters, ship's bells—which quickly cluttered the studio's spacious wooden floor as the cacophonous crew set out to create the song's weird and wonderful aural atmosphere. The cash register that would later ring up Pink Floyd's "Money" appeared from somewhere. An old-fashioned metal bath was dragged in and filled; the Beatles' chauffeur, Alf Bicknell, was assigned a chain to whirl through the water.

And the band begins to play

At the end, the band's road manager, Mal Evans, grabbed a bass drum and led a conga line around this makeshift wonderland of music-making to the collective incantation:

We all live in a yellow submarine
Yellow submarine, yellow submarine

There's a wonderful symmetry here, between the childlike playfulness that filled the studio and the sensibility of the song itself. More than that, the recording session stands as a testament to the song's true intent—an ode to pure fun, nothing more and nothing less. But while fun—the exultant joy of creation—has always been a major animating force of art, it has never been a sufficient raison d'être for art criticism. In one of his beautiful 1930s essays on music, Aldous Huxley—perhaps the patron saint of psychedelics and a prominent paste-up presence in the iconic *Sgt. Pepper's Lonely Hearts Club Band* album cover—remarked on the "absurd multiplicity of attributed 'meanings'" that music can invoke. "Yellow Submarine," due to its nonsensical lyrics and its particular placement in the chronology of the Beatles as odd bedfellow to "Eleanor Rigby" and creative counterpoint to *Revolver,* lent itself to particularly extravagant interpretations, from the sociocultural to the political. One folk magazine took it to be an anti-Vietnam War anthem. The great African American poet, dramatist, and essayist Amiri Baraka saw it as a pathetic paean to white privilege. The English music critic Peter Doggett remarked, "Culturally empty, 'Yellow Submarine' became a kind of Rorschach test for radical minds." (We can put aside for a moment the notion that childlike wonder and sensorial delight amount to cultural emptiness— a lamentable bias that warrants a separate essay.)

This question of the song's meaning reached a crescendo when it was adapted into an animated feature film two years later. What began as a throwaway licensing deal and a mere afterthought for the Beatles became a messy parable of the rift between culture as creative communion and culture as commodity. Before "Yellow Submarine" conquered the airwaves as the highest-grossing single in the UK the year of its release, the Beatles had agreed—or rather, their manager, Brian Epstein, had procured their impetuous agreement—to contribute an original soundtrack and lend their endorsement to a cartoon adaptation by King Features, which had already adapted the life and music of the Beatles into five dozen cartoons. Young painters were recruited from local art schools and an impressive crew of animators, inkers, background artists, and sound engineers was hired from all over the world—Germany, the Netherlands, Australia, Scotland, Spain, the U.S., and all over the UK. As the animation crew worked day and night for eleven months, the Beatles, not quite realizing what they had agreed to, began actively resenting the very idea of the project and treated it like a tedious chore they just had to get out of the way. The film was ultimately finished with very little and very begrudging input from the band.

Its premiere at the London Pavilion in July of 1968 sparked a heightened state of Beatlemania. Fans loved it, most commentators loved it, and even the Fab Four had to admit its charm. But amid the flurry of enthusiasm, the few shrieks of criticism became emblematic of the cultural unease that "Yellow Submarine" sparked—a discomfort with an uninterpretable open-endedness that resists the categorization by which we navigate and process cultural material. The irritation of this unease was best captured by *Daily Mail* entertainment columnist Trudi Pacter, who complained that "the Beatles stubbornly continue to experiment" instead of sticking to the formula that had already proven their music wildly successful. It's a grievance both utterly ridiculous and utterly human: we yearn for art to surprise us, but we also yearn for control, for certitude, for knowing what to expect from those we've come to trust. But what made the Beatles a cultural force was precisely the stubbornness with which they continued to experiment forward into greatness. "Yellow Submarine" was a particularly successful experiment.

Full speed ahead, Ms. Pacter, full speed ahead!

It is precisely this uncomfortable open-endedness of meaning that drove generations of critics to fill the abyss with manufactured meanings. Interpretation, of course, always reveals far more about the interpreter than it does about the interpreted. Just two years before the release of "Yellow Submarine," in her terrific treatise "Against Interpretation," Susan Sontag bemoaned the reactionary "arrogance of interpretation" and called it "the revenge of the intellect upon art."

And yet the interpretation of art is inescapable, and

this might not be such a bad thing after all. "Yellow Submarine," more so than the average song, due to its nonsensical nature, has meant different things to every person who has ever heard it and filled it with subjective sense. It meant different things to my great-grandfather, to my father, and to myself. For the old mathematician, it signified a vitalizing act of intellectual insurgency; for the little boy, a playful and infectious wink at a childhood obsession; for the young man in love, a thread stretching backward and forward in time, connecting him to his childhood self and to the future wife who would beget his own child. And although I, that future child, never got to meet my intellectual insurrectionist great-grandfather, I am linked to him by DNA and by a song from long ago, embedded in my father's synapses and worn note-bare by my mother's lips.

"Once a poem is made available to the public," the teenage Sylvia Plath once wrote to her mother, "the right of interpretation belongs to the reader." It is by this right of interpretation that popular music, popular culture, and perhaps all culture belong to us at all. It is by this right that art is always appropriated by life, that a catchy song with no particular meaning, eavesdropped on by a little boy with his ear pressed to the Iron Curtain, can be woven into a family myth across time and space. This is what popular art does at its best—it provides a screen onto which vastly different people in vastly different circumstances can project the singular meaning of their lives.

AND YOUR BIRD CAN SING

PETER BLAUNER

I'VE LIVED IN NEW YORK CITY my entire life, but on the
night John Lennon was murdered I was in a grubby little
postindustrial ash heap of a Connecticut town, a newly
minted adult working for a newspaper and pretending that
typing up obituary notices made me a writer. Early in the
evening, I'd gone to watch a movie called *Resurrection* in an
empty theater so that I could write a review probably no
one would read about a film that almost no one would see.
Then, feeling homesick, I went to the library and looked for
copies of the *Times* and the *Post*. Why the place was open that
late in a small town, I don't know. A few minutes after I got
there, a homeless guy in a baseball cap with wings on the
sides started screaming and banging on the glass doors. I
went outside to see what was wrong, and for no discernible
reason he punched me in the nose.

I walked back to my rental apartment with a Budweiser
in a bag and dried blood on my chin, and turned on *Monday
Night Football*, trying to figure out if this was what grown-up

life was about. The Patriots and the Dolphins were about to
go into overtime. Then Howard Cosell came on and said
that Lennon had just been shot twice in the back outside the
Dakota apartment building on the Upper West Side, and
was dead at Roosevelt Hospital.

Which didn't make any sense, either.

Well, what could you do with that? A beloved musician
shot dead in front of his home. Assassinated in the city that
helped to make his name—on *The Ed Sullivan Show* and later
at Shea Stadium. My hometown, which he'd adopted as his
own. In the country he'd given solace to when a beloved president was assassinated seventeen years before. Killed in a notoriously violent city by a visitor from beautiful Hawaii. An
absurd end for one of the greatest of all absurdists.

John Lennon made at least half a career out of assault-
ing notions of common sense and propriety. He told the
Queen to rattle her jewelry before he shredded his throat
howling "Twist and Shout" at a famous command performance. He stuck a Coke bottle up his nose in *A Hard
Day's Night*. When asked at a press conference, "How did you
find America?" he replied, "Turn left at Greenland." At the
height of his pop idol fame, he published two books, *In
His Own Write* and *A Spaniard in the Works*, which had sen-
tences like "I was bored on the 9th of Octover 1940 when, I
believe, the Nasties were still booming us led by Madolf
Heatlump (who only had one)." As a child not quite master-
ing the guitar, I took heart from his delight at mangling the

language and hatched the notion of maybe someday trying to play with words of my own.

From that first *Sullivan* appearance, Lennon was my guy in the Beatles. Standing apart from the others, legs bowed, eyes squinting, not taking the business of screaming-teen idolatry too seriously as he chopped away with casual determination at his guitar, as if it hadn't been all that hard to come up with "She Loves You" and "Help!" He wasn't an obvious people-pleaser like Paul, making lover-boy eyes at the camera and shaking his mop for the girls. And he wasn't a studious grind like George, hunched over his Gretsch, making sure to get his Carl Perkins licks just right, before scurrying over to huddle next to Paul at the vocal mike. And he wasn't Ringo, bashing away in the backseat, the ultimate good sport, making sure everyone was having fun and keeping time.

John was more his own man. It wasn't *exactly* that he was aloof or didn't care. His raspy, imperfect voice raged with commitment. But everything about his stance said that he wasn't going to change or adapt for your standards. You had to figure him out, or stay away. *You don't get me* was the implied taunt, before he actually sang the words. And so, "And Your Bird Can Sing" always seemed, to me, the most John Lennon of John Lennon songs.

For some reason, the track was left off the original American release of *Revolver*, so, like a lot of other kids, I discovered it as the theme song for the awful Beatles Saturday-morning cartoon that briefly ran on ABC-TV in the mid-sixties. The show was a crass exercise executed in bad faith with cheap animation, dumb jokes, and excruciating plots about cannibals and karate masters and the like. But even the sight of the cartoon's stiff-limbed, lazy-lidded figures flailing away unconvincingly at their instruments could not diminish the disciplined raucousness, the offhanded invention, the joyous abandon, in the original recording.

It's not a love song, like "I Want to Hold Your Hand" or "If I Fell." Or a bordering-on-hate song, like "You Can't Do That" or "Run for Your Life." It's not a rafter-raiser like "Hey Jude" or a maybe-disguised drug song like "Lucy in the Sky with Diamonds." It's something both more abstract and binding, like an oath to a cause that can't quite be defined.

So what the hell is it about, anyway?

The lyrics start off like a cynical accusation: someone has irked John by claiming to have everything they want. But they won't get him—even though they've seen Seven Wonders and their bird is green. They won't see him or hear him, either. *Wha?* There's also the threat of the "bird" getting broken at some point, and God knows what that portends.

But this isn't an ad hominem attack like Bob Dylan's "Positively 4th Street" (with its Hall of Fame putdown where Dylan says, I wish you could stand in my shoes, so you'd know what a drag it is to see you). Lennon doesn't sound smug or condescending the way Dylan can sometimes. A tentative note of compassion sneaks across the bridge with its sympathetic minor chords and the guitars deconstructing the main riff underneath the vocal. When the target's prized possessions become a burden, Lennon says he'll be around. So is that an offer of friendship? Or a status check? When you're on the way down, I'll still be here. And then there's a hopeful reference to being awakened. But is that a spiritual awakening or a chemical one? Before you can be sure, the break is over, and John has redrawn the battle lines, throwing a final challenge. His target may have heard every sound there is, but hasn't heard him.

And *what about* that music? The band comes crashing in on the first note, firing on all cylinders. If a jet taking off had a tune, it might sound like this. Pounding engines, massive propulsion, a billowing aural fireball pushing off and then the machine improbably soaring. Ringo holds the pattern steady with his snare and hi-hat while John churns up clouds of distortion with his rhythm guitar. Two lead guitars put wings on a melody that might have been a little twee and precious if it wasn't played with such proto-psychedelic aggression. And somewhere amid the beautiful noise, the pilot's voice cuts in, defiant and all-too-human. It took me years to notice that an intricate bass part ties it all together, somehow weaving around the melody while holding down the bottom. Then the song ends on rumbling notes of irresolution that suggest the journey isn't quite over.

It's all done in two minutes, but it feels like you've been around the world. No wonder McCartney made sure to follow it on the original *Revolver* album with one of his best songs, "For No One." This was a time when the Beatles could still play with the force and cohesion of a seasoned live band, but were just beginning to unlock the potential of the modern recording studio as an instrument in the mix.

A few days before, they'd used tape effects and Leslie speakers to assemble a revolutionary brain-melting collage around John's composition "Tomorrow Never Knows." "Bird" doesn't go quite that far. The great musicologist and songwriter Marshall Crenshaw, who once played John in a stage production of *Beatlemania*, identifies it as one of Lennon's "last conventional songs" before he went off on the wild-blue-yonder streak that included "Strawberry Fields Forever," "Being for the Benefit of Mr. Kite," "I Am the Walrus," and "Revolution 9." In its structure and feeling, "Bird" anticipates those later experiments while still rocking as hard as "Dizzy Miss Lizzy" or "I'm Down."

Strangely, though, John himself was less impressed. At various times, he described the song as "another horror" and "another of my throwaways." And when you hear the band's first attempt to record the track, on April 20, 1966, you can hear what he means. He can barely keep from cracking up in the vocal booth with Paul. It's hard to tell if something just happened in the studio or if he's just stoned and overtaken by the nonsense in his own words. One rumor had it that the song was a rejoinder to Frank Sinatra, who'd put down the Beatles and reputedly liked to ask his friends, "How's your bird?"—probably referring to male equipment. But a cursory listen to this early version hints that the real source inspiration was probably the Byrds. George's twelve-string guitar

AND YOUR BIRD CAN SING   93

part sounds like a blatant imitation of Roger McGuinn's trademark Rickenbacker twang, and, when they aren't giggling, John and Paul are striving for a harmony blend reminiscent of McGuinn and Gene Clark.

When I heard this version for the first time on *Anthology 2*, released in 1996, I was a little embarrassed and mystified about why I loved the song so much. The lyrics were close to doggerel, the playing managed to be both desultory and over-busy, the vocals were too strenuous on Paul's part and lackluster on John's. The whole thing was a drag. Perhaps Lennon was right. Not only was the song crap, but maybe the Beatles were just a group imitating other groups. Whatever fondness I had for the record was just nostalgia for childhood that didn't hold up in the harsh light of adulthood.

But then I listened again to the final version they recorded just six days later in the same studio; the bird had somehow taken flight. It was hard to hear where the metamorphosis had come in. The words were virtually the same, the melody was unchanged, and the arrangement was similar. But the song had become a forceful sui generis creation, with all traces of the original influences completely molted away. This could only have been the Beatles, with John Lennon at the forefront, in the full spring bloom of their careers, out of the Cavern and well on the way to Strawberry Fields.

So what happened? How did the thing transform in so short a time?

Obviously the band knew the song better, having run through it exhaustively a few days before, but the performance is completely fresh and committed, as if they're discovering the tune for the first time. Maybe that exuberance is ginned up by studio tricks, hence John's later suspicion of the track. Having helped to fashion the brilliant soundscape of "Tomorrow Never Knows" less than a week before, perhaps producer George Martin and engineer Geoff Emerick felt emboldened to find new ways to fill out the aural canvas for a more "normal" pop song with guitars played through revolving Leslie speakers and a slightly drier-than-usual drum sound. So it could be that part of the track's success is not just as a song written by a composer or two, but as a record.

But what truly makes "Bird" a great quintessential John Lennon song is Paul McCartney. Like a lot of prematurely cynical people, I used to take Sir Paul for granted. Yes, he was a great singer and a great tunesmith, but he was a teacher's pet, a shameless panderer, the self-conscious "cute" one, someone not to be trusted. In the film *Let It Be*, the other members of the group become visibly annoyed and increasingly disaffected by his relentless pushiness and organization, his determination to sit down and *get things done* on his terms. No wonder they broke up right after this. He's like a dad trying to get a bunch of surly children in the car so they can all get where they need to be, while John just wants to hang out with Yoko.

But once you have children of your own, you start to

become more attuned to his point of view. Or at least that's how it was for me after my two sons were born. I learned that you have to become more like Paul so your kids can be free to act more like John. They get to be intuitive and rebellious while you stand by waiting patiently. They amaze you, they come up with wonderful ideas that you could never have thought of, and sometimes they go off in the wrong direction and waste a lot of time. And then you have to shake the keys and lay down the law, telling everyone to get in the goddamn car already or there won't be any party.

Yes, I'm going to say it: Famous as McCartney is, the man is still underrated. Okay, the world knows he wrote and sang "Yesterday," "Penny Lane," "I've Just Seen a Face," and all the others. And anyone with half an ear can tell that his bass playing is the supple spine of most Beatles records. But listen even more closely and you realize that he's the indispensable element in the songs he didn't write or sing lead on, as well. That's his kamikaze guitar tearing into George's "Taxman" and John's "Good Morning Good Morning," his flutelike Mellotron that leads into "Strawberry Fields," and his tape loops and wayward piano contributing to the chaotic wonder of "Tomorrow Never Knows." In his book, *Here, There and Everywhere: My Life Recording the Music of the Beatles*, Geoff Emerick describes Paul staying in the studio long after the others left, perfecting his bass parts and adding the subtle simonizing touches on other instruments that allow those songs to sound as good now as they did when they were recorded more than half a century ago.

McCartney himself says "Bird" was eighty percent John, twenty percent Paul. But that's some twenty percent. The foundation is still John's on the final version, but it's Paul joining George on the harmony guitar intro, giving a necessary touch of raw urgency to the part that Harrison had just played prettily the week before (and saving the riff from sounding like something the Electric Light Orchestra would play on one of their seventies hits). He trims his vocal part, giving John enough room to state his case while chiming in strategically for just a few words at the end of each verse for the crucial amount of sweetening. And then he lays down that monster bass line, which Marshall Crenshaw compares to the crucial element in a Bach invention, the unnoticed piece that locks everything into place.

It's still John's song, but it wouldn't be worth a second listen without what Paul brought to the mix. Or at the very least it wouldn't still sound as rudely alive after a half century without him. Sadly, though, John seemed to rarely return the favor, especially in the later section of the Beatles' career. Maybe it was drugs or personal estrangement, but John retreated from the collaboration, preferring to declare Yoko his true artistic partner as well as his wife. An understandable choice in some ways, although I can't really remember the last time I put on "Don't Worry Kyoko (Mummy's Only Looking for a Hand in the Snow)" or "Sisters O Sisters."

In fact, the older you get and the more you learn about John Lennon, the harder it is not to have complicated feelings about the man. He sang "Love is the answer," but never told his eldest son he loved him. He was, on occasion, abusive toward women. More often, he was ungracious and ungrateful toward his peers and collaborators, discouraging to other musicians and hurling brutal insults toward McCartney in interviews and songs after the band dissolved.

But that's how it is when the child listening to records alone in his room becomes the man playing the same songs in the car for his kids. You realize that your heroes are not just human, but deeply flawed in ways you might find hard to forgive even in a friend. The songs that once defined you, that once meant everything to you, change—whether you want them to or not. You realize that love is definitely *not* all you need, that the narrator of "No Reply" needs a restraining order, and that—as Elvis Costello pointed out—a millionaire has a lot of gall to urge his listeners to imagine no possessions. After a while, you put certain records out on the street and forget the times they got you through. They can't be the same songs, because you're not the same.

But then there are other songs that grow old with you, they reinvent themselves, they evolve and show you sides that even their composers couldn't have imagined, or maybe you just adapt them to the circumstances of your life. And so when I hear "And Your Bird Can Sing" now, I don't hear John Lennon being purposefully obscure and inscrutable anymore. I hear a guy singing to himself, trying to work out his own contradictions. What do you do when your prized possessions weigh you down? How can you feel so alone with friends around you? How can you be well-known and still be unseen? How can you exist in a world that demands compromise and still be your own man (or your own woman)? When he sings "You can't hear me," it doesn't sound like a taunt anymore. There's an undertone of sorrow, maybe even desperation. No wonder the guitars repeat the first few notes of the main riff three times at the end, like a detective knocking on a door. And then it opens, the other instruments drop off, revealing Paul thrumming away softly at his bass after hours, as if mulling a question that can never be answered.

I had the day off from work after Lennon was murdered. My nose had stopped swelling by then and I had access to a Chrysler Cordoba. But I didn't drive down and join the crowds that stood out on West Seventy-second Street under Lennon's apartment window, singing his songs and keeping his widow up. In fact, it was many years before I laid eyes on the Strawberry Fields memorial in Central Park. I never saw the need to visit or to take my kids. Because, for me, John Lennon lives on somewhere else. He talked a good game about coming together and power to the people, but the real spirit of the man exists in a more private place. And I go there whenever I hear this glorious ode to being misunderstood.

TOMORROW NEVER KNOWS

JON PARELES

"TOMORROW NEVER KNOWS" sounded like nothing I'd ever heard. The big, buzzing drone of the tamboura, the Indian instrument that opens the song, wasn't just a sustained note; it was a vast, mysterious environment. The lopsided, sputtering drum pattern that gets louder and busier on the third and fourth beats, and ends with a splash of tambourine, had a peculiar, seemingly mechanized feeling.

And then there were all those swarming, laughing, whistling sounds—seagulls? giant mosquitoes? a phantom calliope?—that race in before John Lennon starts singing, and then come back to taunt him and goad him between his melody lines. Morphing and melting and realigning throughout the song, then gathering around a guitar solo running in reverse, they were like visitations from other dimensions, or a gaggle of noisy ghosts.

Even Lennon's voice, which, by 1966, was a familiar presence on hit radio, was different. It was, as always, buttonholing and insistent. But it was also serene, more pedagogic than confessional or confrontational, more wraithlike; it was as much an aura as a person. On "Tomorrow Never Knows," Lennon had floated above it all.

What was this about? I had no clue—only a growing fascination. I was twelve years old, taking piano lessons and trying to play Bach and Chopin, starting to look afresh at girls and getting my ration of current music from a few Top 40 stations on AM radio. I wouldn't discover free-form FM rock radio for another year, and any drug experiences were even further away. Although "Tomorrow Never Knows" was by the ubiquitous Beatles, it was worlds away from the pop or rock I had known until then.

"Tomorrow Never Knows" would prove to be, like so many Beatles songs, a great predictor of rock to come: a tightly packed bundle of far-reaching implications, a song on which other bands could (and would) build entire catalogs. It also happened to gather sounds and ideas I would be drawn to instinctively, and later—perhaps to justify my pleasures—intellectually.

"Tomorrow Never Knows" invoked the wider world of non-Western music: scales, rhythms, tones, and other parameters that couldn't be mapped onto a piano keyboard or Western music notation. It also exposed the surreal sound manipulations of the recording studio; the psychoacoustic effects of drone, repetition, and noise, and the mutable links between music and spirituality, music and physiology, and/or music and drugs. It was just three minutes long, but it was a revelation: a portal to decades of music to come.

"Tomorrow Never Knows" portends the Velvet Underground, psychedelia and its heirs, ambient music, the post-punk minimalism of Sonic Youth, various sectors of electronic dance music and artier hip-hop, and countless other pieces of music that are richly repetitive and sonically immersive. It's proof—yet hardly the only example in the Beatles catalog—that avant-garde techniques can infiltrate and re-shape pop. That was one lasting lesson I drew from "Tomorrow Never Knows": that pop can encompass the strangest things.

Until they made *Revolver*, the Beatles—and the pop songs around them—had mostly portrayed teen and slightly more grown-up romance, moving through the cycle from infatuation to bliss to breakup to the next liaison. Pop songs did that job with craft and genius in the mid-1960s. In 1965, the number one hits included the Beatles' "Yesterday," Sonny and Cher's "I Got You Babe," the Temptations' "My Girl," and the Righteous Brothers' "You've Lost That Lovin' Feelin'." Songs like those were succinct, emotive, and spectacular—yet still limited in subject and scope.

But there was a watershed change in 1966, the year *Revolver* came out. "Tomorrow Never Knows" wasn't aimed at children like me, nor was it for the shallow teens presumed to be pop's most important consumers. It was made by artists who dared listeners to join them in looking ahead.

That was the year after Bob Dylan went electric at the Newport Folk Festival, an action that told the ascetic folk revival that reaching the world was better—and smarter, and wilder, and deeper—than righteous purism, and that rock had countless ways to grow up and push outward. His example was heeded almost immediately. The year also brought burgeoning literary and musical ambitions (and, no doubt, increasing drug experimentation) to rock. It brought in pretensions, sure—but it brought even more innovation.

The vanguard musicians were World War II babies who happened to be coming into confident adulthood with the support of an ideal mass audience: the baby boomers (a few years older than me), who were heading into their college years and ready to think a little more while they listened, to contemplate a new LP in a haze of pot smoke and speculation. Hail the demographics; what a magnificent difference they made.

The Beatles could easily have had a few more good years of a standard pop career if they had stayed with their Merseybeat rock and roll love songs—the kind that Lennon and McCartney were so good at writing, with instantly memorable tunes and exuberant voices atop slyly sophisticated harmonies. They were pros.

Yet they were pros who refused to become hacks—and who, amazingly enough in the music business then or now, were encouraged to experiment. "Tomorrow Never Knows"—along with the whole *Revolver* album—was the Beatles thinking for themselves and assuming (correctly, as it turned out) that fans would still follow them. It was only three years after "I Want to Hold Your Hand," but in the other songs on *Revolver*, they sang about a lonely old woman, a rapacious taxman, and a peculiar doctor, about materialism and alienation and mortality, more often than they sang about romance.

The lyrics to "Tomorrow Never Knows" were sparked by Lennon reading *The Psychedelic Experience: A Manual Based on the Tibetan Book of the Dead* by Timothy Leary, Richard Alpert, and Ralph Metzner, a book that mapped LSD trips along the lines of Buddhist doctrine. In 1972, Lennon would call "Tomorrow Never Knows" "my first psychedelic song." Mine, too; it was not kid stuff.

The Beatles' music was transforming itself even faster than their lyrics. They had already done wonders with their two guitars, bass, and drums, plus a stray piano or string quartet. But they came to *Revolver* ready to jettison formulas. "Tomorrow Never Knows" was the first song recorded for *Revolver*, even though it ended up closing the album (because, perhaps, what could follow it?). Clearly, the Beatles walked into those sessions brimming with ambition.

Lennon and McCartney were writing most songs separately by 1966. But the Beatles developed them communally, and "Tomorrow Never Knows" was one of the band's synergistic gems, a perfect convergence of individual fixations. This was another lesson I'd later recognize from "Tomorrow Never Knows": the beauty of disparate inputs.

It was a John Lennon song, and his demo of it was already quite odd. Since "Tomorrow Never Knows" stays in one chord throughout, Lennon sang the melody over a loop of guitar and drums he had made with Ringo Starr. The demo, unveiled on *Anthology 2*, is obviously a sketch—shaky and out of phase—but the Beatles and their producer, George Martin, heard potential.

George Harrison had started collecting Indian instruments, including the tamboura he'd use on "Tomorrow Never Knows." Harrison had played a sitar on "Norwegian Wood" on *Rubber Soul* in 1965, but that would be only the beginning of the Beatles' exotic borrowings. Playable by amateurs who merely have to keep plucking its single note, the tamboura is used in Indian raga to provide continuity and a harmonic foundation. Harrison realized that it was the right instrument at the right time when John Lennon arrived with the droning "Tomorrow Never Knows"; the five tones of the song's melody—a C major arpeggio, plus a B-flat—also hint at Eastern modes. The vocal dips down a whole step in lines like "It is not dying," and the recorded track adds the lower chord—B-flat rather than C, using a loop from an orchestral recording—but the drone persists throughout the song.

While Harrison was looking East, McCartney had discovered, via Karlheinz Stockhausen, the sampling aesthetic of *musique concrète*: sounds committed to magnetic tape, looped (with adhesive tape holding the ends together) for infinite repetition and duration, playable forward or backward at any speed, to be abstracted into pure aural sensation. Although tape loops are now a technology that seems utterly prehistoric and kludgy, it was a conceptual leap. Taped sounds no longer had to be documentary; they were just waveforms preserved on magnetic particles, subject to physical handling and electronic alteration. After hearing Lennon's demo, McCartney suggested that the band members make loops and bring them to the studio to be mixed into the song: homework. The tamboura note was also looped, so it could sustain indefinitely.

And what about Ringo Starr's part of the teamwork? For one thing, he devised (with McCartney) and executed that odd, unswerving drumbeat with his usual magnificent steadiness; what sounds mechanical is, by all accounts, hand-played. Starr also, in one of his offhand press conference koans, gave "Tomorrow Never Knows" its title.

With the great serendipity that often inflects a pop career, the Beatles changed recording engineers as they began to make *Revolver*. Geoff Emerick, the new engineer (and later producer for Elvis Costello), cowrote a memoir—*Here, There and Everywhere: My Life Recording the Music of the Beatles*—that music geeks have pored over ever since it appeared. He was willing to bend the institutional rules of the august EMI Studios where the Beatles recorded, and he started working with the band the day they began "Tomorrow Never Knows" and *Revolver*—perfect timing.

By Emerick's account, Lennon said he wanted to sound "like the Dalai Lama chanting from a mountaintop, miles away"—which was not the most practical instruction on microphone placement. Emerick's implementation was to run Lennon's voice through a Leslie: a heavy wooden cabinet holding rotating treble and bass speakers that create a phasing effect by acoustic brute force. Nowadays the Leslie can be emulated by a digital plug-in, but in the analog era the giant physical apparatus was required. The Leslie was made to be paired with a Hammond electric organ to swell and enrich its sound. But after "Tomorrow Never Knows," the Leslie started to be used everywhere. That was another musical lesson for me, soon to be explosively reinforced by Jimi Hendrix: "proper" equipment usage doesn't matter, only the resulting sound.

The more I've learned about "Tomorrow Never Knows," the more I marvel at its Rube Goldberg ingenuity. The Beatles, Martin, and Emerick built that oceanic sound with only four tracks in a few days of sessions. One of those tracks was occupied by the tape loops, mixed in real time in what must have been a wacky scene. According to Emerick, the tape machines in EMI Studios' various rooms were all connected to a mixer and were running the loops simultaneously. EMI technicians in their white lab coats held pencils or drinking glasses inside the loops to provide the right tension, and as they listened to a playback, the Beatles called out which loops to add when, as faders were pushed up and down.

Flesh, muscle, and breath—playing instruments, singing vocals, holding pencils or glasses, turning mixer knobs, giving directions—were involved at every stage of making "Tomorrow Never Knows." As the analog era recedes, this becomes rarer and more—emotionally and literally—touching.

But "Tomorrow Never Knows" was also a harbinger of music's technological future. When I studied electronic music in the early 1970s, using an Arp synthesizer, whose modules filled a studio, tape loops were still state-of-the-art methodology and computers were for experts only. But it wouldn't be long before physical loops gave way to neater, digital iterations. Meanwhile, the sounds of those loops no longer needed acoustic sources, and the esoterica of filters and modulators gave way to easy graphic user interfaces. Where tape loops freed performers from simple physical repetition, digital looping brought more control, and more possibilities, to every parameter of a sound. More control has meant less happy chaos, like the partly random collisions of sounds when the loops go haywire during the guitar solo in "Tomorrow Never Knows." But looping has encouraged the kind of cyclical, hypnotic structures that Lennon (along with the minimalist composers of the 1960s and 1970s) had intuited with "Tomorrow Never Knows." Now, of course, loops are not only the foundation of electronic music, but also the core of countless pop hits.

For me, many Beatles songs are now tinged with nostalgia: for my own youthful innocence, for theirs, for the ways rock was made and heard and transmitted in earlier eras. But "Tomorrow Never Knows" has never become a period piece—it has held its place through fifty years of playlists. It was simultaneously hazy and hardheaded, psychedelic and proto-punk. It was as internally hyperactive as any 1970s jam band, yet also as bristling and monolithic as the punk rock that followed. The drone and squall of New York noise rock had "Tomorrow Never Knows" in its DNA; so did Kraut-rock, and shoegaze, and lo-fi indie rock, and black metal, and every other variant and offshoot involving the glorious mess of overtones generated by a thick acoustic drone. It's only stretching things a little to extrapolate the looping and density of "Tomorrow Never Knows" toward some of hip-hop's sonic collages.

The drone of "Tomorrow Never Knows" was also a sound I would hear in much more ancient music that I had yet to discover and would come to cherish: the drone-loving styles of music from India, Africa, the Middle East, the British Isles, the Balkans, the Americas. Bagpipes, didgeridoos, gamelans. There are abundant pleasures in the tensions and releases, the ambiguities and implications, of harmonic motion; the Beatles certainly knew how to toy with chords. But "Tomorrow Never Knows" revealed to me that stasis can be its own reward.

Meanwhile, the loops—and the whole ambience of "Tomorrow Never Knows"—pointed elsewhere: not only to the entire modern edifice of electronic music, but also to the embrace of mechanization and artificiality across popular music. There's something remote and detached about the sound of "Tomorrow Never Knows," a purposeful abandonment of naturalism. Producers and engineers had long understood that a recording, like a photograph, was never a neutral document of an event, but that was their secret. They usually strove to make a song sound like a preserved performance. And while the Beatles were hardly the first to use the studio as an instrument, "Tomorrow Never Knows" (and, in its wake, the rest of *Revolver*) got aggressively unreal.

It wasn't just Lennon's vocal tone and the incursions of those madcap loops. Emerick also did some decidedly non-standard close-miking and compression of the drums (and, trivia fans know, he deadened the bass drum by stuffing the eight-armed sweater from the cover of *Help!* inside it). Later, out of nowhere, the end of the song sprinkles on some whimsical, inexplicable honky-tonk piano noodlings. The real-time parts of the song—vocals, drums, McCartney's subtly pulsing bass—are no more prominent in the mix than the studio artifacts. We take for granted now that pop recordings are fantasies and fabrications, but "Tomorrow Never Knows" was early in flaunting it.

That air of illusion, that otherworldliness, ties in directly to Lennon's lyrics. Truth be told, and despite the fact that I would become a writer, I didn't pay much attention to the words of "Tomorrow Never Knows" for many years. If I thought about them at all, I took them to be some sort of drug allusion, or maybe just more of Lennon's paradox-loving jabberwocky side, precursors to the singable conundrums of "I Am the Walrus." It took some later education, and the growing accumulation of Beatles lore, to make it clear that Lennon was echoing Buddhist beliefs about meditation, detachment from the self, infinite love, enlightenment, and cycles of reincarnation—which are, after all, another kind of loop.

But for me, the philosophy had always been contained in

the sound of the song: its drone and undulation, its separation from the mundane, the tranquillity that it somehow created amid its own noise. "Lay down all thoughts, surrender to the void," Lennon intoned, and on four tracks recorded in a few days in 1966, "Tomorrow Never Knows" could make that happen.

LUCY IN THE SKY WITH DIAMONDS

THOMAS BELLER

CHILDHOOD

Mine

MY EARLIEST MEMORIES of the Beatles are wrapped up with the family in whose company I first heard the band. Not my own family—who preferred classical music—but another family who lived down the hall. Brian's family. When we met, I had a mother and a father, and Brian had a sister and two parents who lived together.

In the first years of our friendship we were part of a gaggle of kids in the building who saw one another in the playground and sometimes in one another's apartments. Gradually, an affinity grew between me and Brian—maybe it was as simple as his living on my floor—and when I was around ten or so I started spending more time at his place. Sometimes, less frequently, he came to mine. I know of his visits not from memory but from a photograph—Brian sitting on the lower bunk of my bunk bed, bangs across his forehead. His freckled, pale face looks at the camera with what at the time I would have thought of as a kind of inscrutable blankness that overtook him now and then, one of his moods. When I saw the photo recently, he seemed like a kid with some kernel of sadness in him. Maybe that was part of what drew us together. Neither of us had the faintest idea where this kernel within us came from, or into what frightening form it would blossom. But we both had a sense something was going on.

Our apartments had different views. His apartment faced west, with a soaring view over the park, the highway, the Hudson River. My apartment faced north, looking out over a canyon of brownstones and shorter apartment buildings. It was a rooftop view, expansive, dotted by water towers.

The views inside were different, too. My apartment had paintings with frames, often heavy, with an inside boundary, as though the painting was a jewel to be protected. There were drapes, a baby grand piano, a gold-hued sofa, antique rugs on the floor. Brian's apartment was also filled with art, but it was new art. Freshly painted canvases composed in wild flourishes by his father, who had converted the living room into a studio. The finished canvases stood stacked against the wall. No frames. Sometimes I would flip through them like they were a deck of playing cards. The paintings were cosmic visions of people dancing through space or faces emerging from waves. New Age fantasies before there was such a term. His work became popular in the sixties and has remained popular.

The feeling of newness at Brian's place extended to everything: push-button phones, an egg-shaped chair with orange upholstery, a stereo connected to a light box that pulsed different colors in time to the music. There was a meditation closet. The family had its own swami. The wood floors had been painted white.

Was Brian my best friend? It's hard to answer that. Friends from the building are a category of their own, set apart from the world of school or camp. We spent most of the hothouse days of our friendship—around the ages of eleven to fourteen—together at his house. I was over there a lot. I joined his family on trips. Sometimes to Chinatown for Sunday dim sum. Sometimes farther afield. It was in this world, in this context, that I had my first sustained exposure to the Beatles.

This was the mid-1970s. I heard the Beatles everywhere. They were a kind of semipermanent part of the aural environment. As a very little kid I didn't even know what a band was. Then, once I understood that this was music made by four guys, I was shocked to discover that they were English. I could detect no accent in their singing voices. It wasn't until I heard them speak that I had this epiphany.

BEATLES SONGS HAVE within them a childishness that goes beyond their pleasing melodies. Their songs are child-friendly. This is obviously true of songs like "Yellow Submarine" and "Maxwell's Silver Hammer," but it is true of many other songs as well that seem to be rocking and sexual: "Please Please Me," "A Hard Day's Night," and especially "I Saw Her Standing There."

These songs are so playful and exuberant, and there is something total in the harmonies—both the notes and the intensity of the singing—that reflects the totality with which children throw themselves into moods or activities. Listening to them now, I can hear within them a sense of danger and sexual adventure, but as a kid I had no clue. A sense of menace or dissonance creeps in at the edges of some of these songs but never takes over. The obvious way to account for this is the dialectic between Paul, who insists you admit it is getting better, and John, who provides the deliciously succinct retort—"It couldn't get much worse."

BRIAN'S MOTHER WAS very beautiful, blond, exuberant, and a little distant. She was American. I would never have been able to put this into words at the time, but among Brian and my parents she was the only one to be born in America. The other three were Jewish refugees uprooted by World War II.

In contrast to his mother's sharp beauty, Brian's father was handsome, but his charisma was harder to define. He was a man who made his own rules. He wore white painter's pants and white T-shirts, juxtaposed against his long black hair and a heavy black beard. He had a big smile with huge white teeth. A slender, muscular body. A lot of yoga. Like the Beatles he had become a success without appearing to reach for it, and made a degree of fun out it—somewhere in the apartment there was a picture of him with a Rolls-Royce that he had decorated with wallpaper or stickers, as the Beatles had done. When I was driving to Chinatown with them it was in an orange Volkswagen station wagon. They had a sauna right in their apartment, wedged in next to the kitchen. Brian and I used it all the time for a brief period, when it was new, and then never again.

That sauna is now used for storage. It has been for decades. Sometimes, during the long visits to my mother's apartment with my family, I sit on the bench across the street and look up at the windows of the building, my eyes searching for the one peculiarly shaped window of that sauna. I can make out the boxes stacked in there. I close my eyes and remember what it was like to be in there with Brian in the heat, at night, the river spread out cold and gray beneath us.

Their place was a duplex. The downstairs half was the one on my floor. I remember when they first built the spiral staircase that led from one floor the other. They cut a perfect little hole in the ceiling and then a narrow spiral staircase was built. All white. Upstairs, you simply stepped into the spiral staircase and descended, but on the lower floor there was an enclosure, a kind of glass box with a door, so that you

would have to open the door to step into that spiral staircase. I think its purpose was to create a separation between
the downstairs, where Brian's dad had some people working
for him, and the upstairs, where they lived—all except Brian,
who had his bedroom downstairs. It was a surreptitious
world down there after hours, with everyone gone, a good
place for young boys. Upstairs was brightness, the living
room converted to a giant painting studio with stereo speakers, though his dad often used headphones. He would dance
in front of his canvases, wearing the headphones, moving
his brush. But other times, he'd play music on the speakers,
often the Beatles.

I WAS ALWAYS CASTING a wild eye at various mothers and
older sisters of my friends. Brian's mother was blond and
very pretty, a beauty queen. In my fantasies about her—when
I was a teenager—she was suffering, somehow, aggrieved, upset, and my hand reached out to gently move the spaghetti
strap of her tank top off her shoulder, slide it off and leave
the shoulder bare. One shoulder, then the other. Like peeling
a fruit. By the time these thoughts entered my mind I had
known her for years in all innocence. It was shocking to me
when I realized, many years later, that I had married a
woman who looked like her.

Once, I saw them fighting. He was in his white painter's
pants and T-shirt. Her back was to me, but I could see how
emphatically she spoke from the way her hair moved, the

tightness in her upper back. It was downstairs, at the base of the spiral stairs, and they were in the glass box. I had pushed the door open without ringing the bell, en route to Brian's room. They were too involved and didn't see me. I could still hear their raised voices. I saw him, gesturing, yelling. I froze, watching.

There was something fiercely intimate about them fighting.

Not long after that, she moved out.

HAD MY FATHER DIED by then? I don't know. That is now the enormous footnote that looms over, or under, those first years of friendship with Brian when I was seven, eight, nine— my dad was sick with cancer. He didn't show it, but it was in him, dormant. I didn't know about it but my parents did. Did this inform my eagerness to get out of the house and down the hall?

Brian's mom now lived in another apartment, just a few blocks away. Brian's sister moved in with her. Brian stayed at his dad's place.

It's crazy to say this but on some level I thought of my friend's dad as an extension of the Beatles. As I mentioned, the family had their own swami. Brian's dad, before he had the full beard, had a heavy mustache. It was as though he had gone through the same metamorphosis of facial hair that the Beatles had from the Red Album to the Blue one.

———————

THE BEATLES ALWAYS seemed so friendly—with "Help!" and "I Want to Hold Your Hand," and even "A Hard Day's Night"—but then at some point I heard another side, something disturbing and problematic. I was interested to discover, recently, in my reading about Lennon, of his struggles as a kid separating reality from fantasy, because I felt like that, too: experience rushing by harmoniously and then not, but always having the feeling of being perched at the edge of a dream, or a game, with some other thing, forbidding, lurking at the edges.

My epiphany about the Beatles took place in an apartment, with a family, who in their own way provided me with another version of that same epiphany, and at around the same time—that everything was not fine, and that into a brightly colored fantasy, a dream of wonder, a kind of Eden, could crawl a libidinous snake. If I had to pick one song that most embodied this feeling that all was wonderful and also frightening, it would be "Lucy in the Sky with Diamonds."

THEIRS

The toilet paper at Abbey Road studios, where the Beatles recorded *Sgt. Pepper's Lonely Hearts Club Band*, was stamped PROPERTY OF EMI. This detail drifted by as part of a listing of the instrumentation on one of the songs on *Sgt. Pepper*. It is unclear to me if every single sheet had these words somehow embossed on it so that unspooling it would create a parade of the repeated phrase, or if it was merely stamped on the packaging for each roll.

READING ABOUT THE BEATLES, I was reminded about how strict and authoritarian British society was at the start of the 1960s and also how recording artists were condescended to. The really famous ones had a kind of power, but they were seen by the record companies, and maybe everyone else with a corporate interest in them, as entertainers, a form of puppets—naive, and requiring manipulation. It's important to remember that all those blues musicians worshipped by the Beatles and the Rolling Stones were completely and utterly ripped off by the businesspeople handling their affairs. This turned out to also be true of the Beatles and the Rolling Stones.

What strikes me now, thinking about this toilet paper (whose subliminal message is . . . what? "You can't even wipe your own ass without us?"), is how much of the humor and adventure of the Beatles' innovations came from their insistence on tweaking the rigidity of the establishment. This included the music business, of course, but also, more generally, the brittle world of English propriety.

SGT. PEPPER'S LONELY HEARTS CLUB BAND is widely viewed as a turning point in the role of the album as a work of art, a great leap forward. But it happened when they looked back to their childhoods. They were thinking about childhood. They had stopped touring. They had turned inward, backward. Away from the bright flashing bulbs, the shrieks. Their live performances had been encased in cascading waves of hysteria. Devin McKinney captures the darker side of Beatlemania in his book *Magic Circles* when he refers to a moment in the movie *A Hard Day's Night* when Ringo is happily drumming along and he suddenly jerks his head away from two creeping schoolgirl fingers: "It is a reflex move of terror and self-protection."

All of *Sgt. Pepper* is imbued with the feeling of childhood, as is the pair of songs that preceded it by three months—"Penny Lane" and "Strawberry Fields," released as a double A-side.

Lennon and McCartney had very different childhoods, colored by very different palettes, and these songs establish the dual tracks that they would take into the subject of childhood: the deep blue suburban skies of "Penny Lane" versus the ambiguous, even sinister, undertones of "Strawberry Fields." But the genius and luck of Lennon and McCartney's collaboration was in the interplay of these moods.

"Strawberry Fields" alludes to an orphanage from Lennon's childhood. That fact alone colors that song and its lyrics darkly, but it was yet another shock for me when I learned the exact circumstances in which John Lennon was reared: his father abandoned the family; his mother abandoned him, giving him to an aunt to raise. All this by the age of five or six.

George Martin later remarked that excluding "Strawberry Fields" and "Penny Lane" from *Sgt. Pepper* was "the biggest mistake of his life." Such a fantastically melodramatic remark from the usually understated Martin. I wonder why he felt so strongly.

Perhaps it was because the theme of childhood, felt so powerfully in *Sgt. Pepper*, would've been accented and illuminated even further by the inclusion of those two childlike, child-centric songs. Or maybe it was that he felt the songs were somehow never given their due by virtue of being stranded on a single. Was his regret about what the album lost from their exclusion, or was his regret due to what the two songs lost in recognition? I think he felt them to be part of the overall statement of the album, and that the songs, for all their sales, had been stranded.

HERS

For days I have been listening to *Sgt. Pepper*, the whole album, straight through. It feels like a kind of novel in dreamscape, with one song leading to the next. For a while, I was less enamored with "Lucy in the Sky with Diamonds" than with the songs just before and after. At one point I am delighted to realize that I am patching a hole where the rain comes in while listening to a song on just this subject. I pay extra attention to "Lucy in the Sky with Diamonds," and after playing it many times I come to like it more. But my feelings about it remain ambiguous.

Then one day I decide to play it for my daughter during our morning drive to school.

Nine years old. Blond, like her mother. Like her brother. In shorts. Rain pours down in sheets. The car moves through a gray murk of wilderness that is the school rush hour of uptown New Orleans.

"What do you think of the song?" I ask once it has gotten through the opening and the first chorus.

"I hate it."

"Why?" I say.

"Because it's boring."

"Why?"

"Because it's stupid."

"Why?"

"Because it's not Taylor Swift."

"If you had to describe it," I ask, "what would you say?"

"I would say it was boring."

"What else would you say?"

"I would say it was stupid and boring."

"But you like things that are not Taylor Swift."

"Yep. But I don't like this song."

Epic rain, epic puddles. Rolling Thunder.

"Look at this," I say, and plow through a vast puddle of unknown depth.

She allows a flicker of pleasure on her face. So smart, so pretty, so difficult, so lovely, and she is only nine. Nine!

"When I woke up this morning I thought it was still night," she says. "It was so dark."

The oak trees stretch across the avenue, crowd the streets. The rain pelts us violently.

"Let me ask you a question: Do you think . . ."

"You just asked me a hundred questions, and they were all stupid!"

"This!" I say. "This part of the song. Listen." It's the part of the song when that gorgeous waterfall of chorus washes over at the end of the perky part of the chorus, the "Lucy in the sky with diamonds" part, that long *Ahhhh, ahhhhh*.

"Don't you think this part of the song is like candy?" I ask when the part ends.

"No."

"What about this part—isn't it like a fairy tale?"

"Yeah, but it's still stupid."

"But sometimes you like fairy tales, right?"

"Not in this song."

"Describe it. Give me a word."

"Creepy."

I PULL UP to the entrance of her school and my daughter moves away from the car with stiff-legged haste. The heavy rain falls on her blond hair, darkening it. The determination with which she makes this transition from being with me in the car, an extension of home, to the public world of school always amuses me. I yell out—half to torment her and half to remind her—"Have a great day, gorgeous. I love you!"

Then I make my way home through the lush, springtime streets of New Orleans. She had been in such a bad mood, so cranky, I am glad to have her out of the car. The hard rain is now letting up. The sky is still a dark gray, backlit. The world becomes dewy and mysterious.

Suddenly, I'm inside a song where my future life is being narrated in the most chilling terms, except I am no longer fixing a hole where the rain comes in. She is leaving home. The story of a girl who has snuck out on her parents and vanished, told from the point of view of the parents. I absorb the song in a state of incredible, building grief. When the parents sing about giving her everything money could buy, I detect an element of mockery. How could they be so naive? There is the sense that the parents have been putting on a show for the benefit of their daughter, which echoes the whole conceit of showmanship around which *Sgt. Pepper* is built.

I TOGGLE BETWEEN wondering if there's contempt in the voices of Lennon and McCartney as they embody these grief-struck parents in the morning, that mother in particular, clutching a letter and crying out in weeping grief, "She's leaving us." And I'm wondering if my nine-year-old is gone already.

Let me be clear: I am very close to this girl. I love this girl! She loves me. We do things together. We've been planning on making a concrete planter, a household project for the garden, for which she has a tremendous enthusiasm.

It's not entirely clear to me if she really cares about the concrete planter. It might be that she likes watching the videos of how to make a concrete planter with me before she goes to bed. That enthusiasm for the concrete planter may just be a kind of instrument that she has learned to play so as to extend the episode of watching a video before sleep. It's better than lying in the dark.

By the end of "She's Leaving Home," I'm quite distressed. And then that absolutely cutting remark, about those things inside so long denied "for so many years."

I drive back to our leaky house. I listen to the Elton John version of "Lucy in the Sky with Diamonds." It's only one of two Beatles covers to go to number one on the American charts ("With a Little Help from My Friends" by Joe Cocker is the other). Elton John gives the song a wholesomeness that the original lacks, inflicting upon it a vague feeling of nostalgia that he puts on many of his songs, encasing them like a gloss. The chorus, that modulated *Ahhh*, lacks the sublime colors of the Beatles' song. The biggest change, however, is the way that the opening verses, with their marmalade skies, have been denuded of that half-chanted creepiness. Elton John made the song much less weird.

The Beatles version is off-putting, psychedelic, and sublime, "magic and talismanic," Wilfrid Mellers, the Beatles scholar, called it. Mellers thought the song was "a revocation of the dream world of childhood." But for me, it isn't so much a revocation of the dream world of childhood as the articulation of both sides of the fence—between reality and fantasy, between the lush optimism of the chorus and the uncertain, almost deranged sound of the verse. Between staying within the world of innocence and parents and family, and taking a trip, leaving home on your own terms, before time, or some unexpected circumstance, takes it from you.

SHE'S LEAVING HOME

MONA SIMPSON

"SHE'S LEAVING HOME" opens with a solo harp sequence, played by Sheila Bromberg, the first female musician ever on a Beatles album. Ms. Bromberg later claimed she was paid only nine pounds for her contribution; not so surprising, perhaps, for a recording made in 1967. (One wonders how the male string players were compensated.) Paul, she said, made her play the bars again and again. Finally, the session players packed up their instruments at midnight and left because they had other jobs in the morning. When Ms. Bromberg heard the final version, she realized the Beatles had picked her very first take.

It's an arresting, showy flourish of rippling strings, repeated twice before any human voice is heard.

After the harp solo, the narrative starts, with Paul singing. We learn that it's dawn, five o'clock in the morning.

He tells a simple story of a girl coming downstairs, leaving a note for her parents, and going out the back door, accompanied by a majestic swell of strings.

The girl seems smaller, overwhelmed by all the strings, with their classical portent.

PAUL McCARTNEY SAID, "John and I wrote 'She's Leaving Home' together. It was my inspiration. We'd seen a story in the newspaper about a young girl who'd left home and not been found, there were a lot of those at the time, and that was enough to give us a story line. So I started to get the lyrics: she slips out and leaves a note and then the parents wake up . . . It was rather poignant."

There were a lot of those at the time . . .

The runaway—the runaway girl in particular—was a known type in the sixties and seventies. I once attended, with my mother, a benefit dinner for a home dedicated to the reformation of what were then called "incorrigible girls." These girls, already living with nuns, who were presumably more equipped than the girls' families to contain them, had made the centerpieces for the benefit tables; Christmas trees crafted from *Reader's Digests*, the pages folded into triangles, fanned out and then spray-painted, and candlesticks sculpted from melted-down LPs, the hole at the center repurposed for a taper.

THE NEWSPAPER ARTICLE Paul McCartney read had appeared in the London *Daily Mail* on February 27, 1967, with the headline "A-Level Girl Dumps Car and Vanishes." The runaway's name was Melanie Coe and she was seventeen. Her father was quoted as saying, "I cannot imagine why she should run away, she has everything here."

The song was recorded over two days in mid-March (the 17th and 20th), less than a month later.

"I LIKED IT AS A SONG," Paul McCartney said in *1000 UK Number One Hits*, by Jon Kutner and Spencer Leigh, "and when I showed it to John, he added the long sustained notes, and one of the nice things about the structure of the song is that it stays on those chords endlessly. Before that period in our songwriting we would have changed chords but it stays on the C chord. It really holds you. It's a really nice little trick and I think it worked very well. John was doing the Greek chorus, the parents' view: 'We gave her most of our lives, we gave her everything money could buy.' I think that may have been in the runaway story, it might have been a quote from the parents."

THE CHORUS WORKS as a collective lament, the voice of the parental generation. It begins right after the girl steps outside, before her mother even discovers she's gone, and is repeated three times, with a variation in last repetition. The lyrics contain a familiar generational pathos: "We gave her everything money could buy . . . / We struggled hard all our lives to get by," the rhyme chiming with the final soft "Bye Bye."

Apparently, according to Songfacts.com, the lyrics were inspired by the sayings of John Lennon's aunt Mimi, who raised him after his parents separated. One could imagine him using Mimi's phrasing in "everything money could buy" and "struggled hard all our lives to get by."

THE GIRL'S PARENTS are conventional and fusty. (There were a lot of those at the time, too.) We know this because of the mother's dressing gown, and from the fact that she calls her husband "Daddy" and her presumably teenage daughter "our baby."

But the lyrics don't tip into parody. We hear the parents' anguish, but it doesn't seem excessive, given the circumstances.

Then we're told what the parents don't yet know. That two days later, at nine o'clock (the two chronologies in the 229-word song nicely providing closure), the girl is meeting a man "from the motor trade." A car salesman, do they mean?

THE REAL-LIFE MODEL, Melanie Coe, didn't meet a man from the motor trade (that was made up, Paul claimed, as was the sea captain from "Yellow Submarine"). After she went missing without her car or checkbook, she moved into an apartment in Paddington with a croupier she'd met in a nightclub.

WHEN *SGT. PEPPER'S LONELY HEARTS CLUB BAND,* the album on which "She's Leaving Home" was included, came out in 1967, my mother went downtown to the record store after work and bought it. We lived in Green Bay, Wisconsin, in an apartment we were both proud of. My mother set the vinyl disc on the turntable and played it on our stereo in the white-walled living room. (*White walls with a kid!* her sister and mother had said, not as a question.)

My mother was thirty-six and I was ten. We bracketed the band. Neither of us fit into their generation exactly, but we were close enough to consider ourselves kindred spirits, wild fans.

We danced around the living room in our socks.

MELANIE COE'S PARENTS found her ten days after the newspaper article appeared and brought her home to have an abortion. But the parents of the girl in the song must have feared the worst: murder, rape, drugs, total estrangement. Those fears for runaway girls were on our minds in those days.

In the song, things are less dire. None of the terrors materialize, not even estrangement. (The girl feels a twinge leaving, wishing her note had said more.) The chorus makes sure we feel sympathy for the fusty parents in their awful robes who have struggled all their lives to get by.

With all the classical ballast and portentous strings fore-boding tragedy, the grandeur of the wide sweep and the seventh and ninth chords, the song turns on one word. The punch line of the song is not a needle in an arm, a rape, or any of the terrors spooking the culture in 1967. The word *fun* is the linchpin of the song. Fun is the one thing that money can't buy, the thing the poor parents have certainly not had enough of, and the thing their daughter is having right now (if briefly) with the man in the motor trade.

THE AMERICAN COMPOSER Ned Rorem described "She's Leaving Home" as "equal to any song that Schubert ever wrote." When Paul McCartney visited Brian Wilson of the Beach Boys in L.A. in April 1967 to preview *Sgt. Pepper*, he played "She's Leaving Home" on the piano for him and his wife. "We both just cried," Wilson said. "It was beautiful."

FOR ME?

IT WOULD BE YEARS before I met an actual runaway. Her name was Dawn and she was the girlfriend of a friend's older brother. She had more or less moved in with the family. My friend's mom complained about her and my friend agreed: Dawn wanted the comforts of a nice home but didn't want the responsibilities. Laundry, my friend's mom meant. And babysitting. I nodded in agreement, even though I didn't have to do laundry and there was no one to babysit at my house.

At age ten, I found the song haunting. I'd been to that dinner for incorrigible girls. I'd seen pictures of hippies in San Francisco. Already, a girl I was friends with wanted to make out on a bed in our basement "for practice."

But at ten, "Everything money could buy" sounded pretty good to me.

I thought that *I* wouldn't have run away from that.

But then again, I wasn't the runaway type.

GOOD DAY SUNSHINE

JOSEPH O'NEILL

IN THE SUMMER OF 1966, my father, an employee of Chicago Bridge & Iron Company, was assigned to a project in South Africa. The client was African Explosives & Chemical Industries; the job was to build spheres and distilled-water tanks in Umbogintwini on the Natal coast. He flew south, via Athens, from Beirut, and my mother and we three children accompanied him.

Our South African adventure, which lasted a year, belongs almost completely to the earliest, unrecollectable portion of my childhood—the tasteless filter of memory's cigarette. I have kept from that episode only a single visual memory: a very blue ocean and a very blue sky seen from some high-up balcony or window. There seems to be an esplanade or road at the bottom of the image. This vista belonged either to the seaside apartment we finally settled into, which was in Amanzimtoti, or to the hotel on the Bluff in Durban where, upon our arrival in the Republic, we lived as transients. My older sister, Ann, who has an excellent autobiographical memory, clearly recalls that Durban spell, even though it occurred when she was three and a half years old. Specifically, she remembers looking under the hotel bed and finding something left behind by the room's previous occupants: an album.

This extraordinary article—the first of its kind to make its way into our hands; we weren't a musical family— fascinated my sister as a graphic thing. She spent many hours marveling over the cover's nearly nonsensical black-and-white images, and she tells me that I did, too. A drawing of four long-haired heads dominated the white square jacket, and in between the heads, and in the strands of the hair, and even in one of the ears, a strange and impish multitude cavorted. What kind of hobgoblin gathering was this? Why did photographed eyes look out of the line-drawn eyes? It was spooky and delightful and wondrous. The disc itself must have been a marvel; and to extract any LP from its sleeve, one half century and several audio-technological revolutions later, is to reencounter a mysterious astronomical beauty. The small spindle hole is a kind of cosmic hole around which a ringed plane of dark matter whirls. One handles, as my sister and I handled, a starless and ominous spiral galaxy.

My parents, it ought to be mentioned, have no recollection of this discovery and are doubtful about it, and they also have good memories. But neither can they explain how the album, *Revolver* by the Beatles, came into our possession. I trust my sister on this one, and not just because the family's arrival in South Africa roughly coincided with the release of *Revolver* in August 1966. In this field, she has special standing: she was the first in the family to believe that music was important, and her album collection was my earliest persistent source of pop.* In any case, it seems right that the album's origin remain something of a mystery, because this corresponds to the mystery of the music itself. *Revolver* seems to have come into the world from nowhere.

We kept the album, but we had no means of playing it. It wasn't until 1970, after the family had relocated itself and its belongings, first to Lourenço Marques and then to Mersin and then to Kermanshah and finally to The Hague; after my parents and Ann and I had run into Paul and Linda McCartney at Peter Jones in London (they were buying shoes for their little girl, who I deduce must have been the young Heather McCartney); and after the Beatles had broken up— it was not until then that my parents at last bought a record player. It was a Philips, with excitingly stereophonic wooden speakers you could snap down onto the turntable to conjure a heavy but portable wooden box. At last we got to listen to our first album; and I got to hear, for the first time, the song that has always struck me as the album's opening track, even though it opens side two and not side one

---

*I remember Stevie Wonder, Bread, Rod Stewart, Johnny "Guitar" Watson, Jim Croce, Bob Dylan. My parents did own and on occasion play LPs of their own, among them the Dubliners' *At Home with the Dubliners*, Vivaldi's *Le Quattro Stagioni*, an album by Ray Conniff and the Ray Conniff Singers, a greatest hits album by Frank Sinatra, and, most memorable of all, Mikis Theodorakis's *Mauthausen Trilogy*.

(which kicks off with "Taxman," a guitaristically ground-breaking but decidedly overcast number about paying too much tax). I'm referring, of course, to "Good Day Sunshine."

As its title suggests, the song celebrates the good that is solar light. It is a musical bonanza of greeting, morning, and beginning. Long a favorite, apparently, of astronauts waking up in space, it is aural rocket fuel. This jump-starting power is pretty much the whole point of "Good Day Sunshine." Although it is by no means the best or most interesting thing on *Revolver*, its cheerful propulsiveness is unmatched. After a short, cunningly suspenseful basso opening—a discus thrower's windup—the song hurls itself, and us, straight into the famous eponymous three-word chorus. Two minutes later, we're done. The Beatles loved ditties, and "Good Day Sunshine" is a great ditty.

Here I will err. My error will be to analyze the song—to disassemble a gloriously whole acoustic thing in order to relate to it intellectively. To make matters worse, I'm a musicological ignoramus and so have no choice but to confine my analysis to the song's words: an act of formal vandalism, because "Good Day Sunshine" isn't a text you read at length, it's something you listen to in real time. But to err is to wander off in the wrong direction, and wrong directions can be interesting. I never knew, until I erroneously gave the lyrics of "Good Day Sunshine" my full analytic attention, that the more closely one reads them, the more closely they resemble a poem by John Donne.

THESE LYRICS ARE, of course, irreproducible here on account of the crazy avarice and paranoia of the copyright
owners. But we can disclose, with a reasonable measure of
legal safety, that the first verse involves the following sequence of assertions:

1. The first-person protagonist ("P") has a need for
   laughter.
2. The sun being out is a good reason for P to laugh.
3. Being out in the sun makes P feel good.
4. The good feeling in question is a special one.
5. P is in love and the day is a sunny one.

This verse seems to be simply indicative, that is, a collection of statements about the here and now. But upon examination, we see that it offers a psychological conjecture
(about laughter); posits a future state of affairs (sunshine);
makes predictions about how P will feel should this state of
affairs materialize; and, finally, offers a scenario in which
P is in love and in sunshine. (Because there is a comma,
rather than a period, between assertions 4 and 5, it is clear
that the love and sunshine in question are imagined, not experienced.) Beneath their cloak of immediacy, the lyrics operate in what grammarians call the irrealis moods—the iffy
moods of fantasists and theorists. This explains the song's

complex dreaminess. More obviously, it sets in motion its central drama: Will P find the sunny love he seeks?

In verse two, everything lurches from the hypothetical to the actual. A plot materializes. Persons referred to in the first person plural—P and one other, we guess—are taking a walk. It is sunny. When P's feet touch the ground, the ground burns his/her feet.*

We cannot pass over this last detail. A person who walks on burning ground is a firewalker. Firewalking, usually on hot embers or hot stones, is important in many cultures. It can serve as a test of courage and even of culpability, and it almost always functions as a symbolic passage from one state of being, or from one status, to another. Thus understood, "Good Day Sunshine" gives us a protagonist undergoing a painful, courageous, possibly ritualistic transition. But what kind of transition? In suspense, we listen to the final verse. In which:

1. P and one or more others ("we" is used) "then" lie down.
2. They do so beneath a tree that's "shady."
3. P loves "her."†
4. P perceives that she "[i]s loving" him.‡

---

*P's gender is as yet uncertain.
†*At last* we are told that P's companion is female.
‡Note my use of the masculine pronoun. Because P is romancing a woman, we can *presume* P is a man. Unless there are reasons to think otherwise (e.g., the work is by Boy George or Grace Jones or David Bowie or Lady Gaga or anyone else with an artistic or personal interest in normative disruption), a *presumption* of heterosexual and cisgender normativity applies *by convention* to the construction

5. P perceives that she feels "good."
6. P perceives that she "knows" that she is "looking fine."
7. P is very "proud" to "know" that the woman is his possession—"mine," as he puts it.

Note that only *after* the firewalk does P lie down with the woman. On the basis that the firewalk is significant (why else would the song mention it?), the following may be construed: (1) P's firewalk functions as a test and/or proof of his ardor (from the Latin *ardere*, "to burn"), and (2) having passed this test of fire, he, and indeed she, can move to the next stage of their romance: lying under a "shady" tree.

What a site of nuance this is!* "Shady" connotes questionable honesty or legality, so there immediately arises the possibility, as surely there arises in any romantic situation, of double-dealing and/or an emotional tort. However: the tree, precisely because it's "shady," screens the couple from the sun's rays. P can therefore ascertain if, *absent the gladdening effect of sunshine*, he nonetheless feels joy; and because he does so feel, he can deduce that his companion is the source

---

of pop lyrics. (The Kinks' transgender classic "Lola" depends on this convention in order to upend it.) Of course, many listeners of "Good Day Sunshine" will suppose from the get-go that P is male and straight on the basis that the song's vocalist, Paul McCartney, is male and straight. The sexual and gender identification of artist and artistic protagonist is another conventional presumption: see Claudine Longet's 1967 cover of "Good Day Sunshine," in which P is a woman and her companion a man. All that said, I don't doubt there are, or soon will be, LGBT versions of "Good Day Sunshine." Nothing in the lyrics precludes it.
*"Nuance" derives from the French *nuer*, "to shade," which itself comes from *nue*, "cloud"—sunshine's perennial antagonist.

of his joy.* The shady tree therefore offers a second test of P's feelings for the woman—and the test is passed. He is able to declare: *She* makes me feel good, not the sunshine. P loves *her*.

We find ourselves, we realize, in the realm of courtly love; and this permits us to recognize something that should have been instantly apparent. By removing her from sunlight to tree shade, from an exposed place to a screened space, the man has escorted the woman from peril to safety. A third chivalrous deed has been accomplished. Surely that is enough, one might think, to *win her favor*? I use, and indeed italicize, this phrase, not only in order to echo the terminology of a medieval romance but also to remind us that "win" originates from a fusion of the Old English *winnan* (to labor, strive, fight) and *gewinnan* (to conquer, take possession of). Little wonder, then, that P describes his romantic happiness in terms of the proprietorial satisfaction: He feels "proud" that the woman is his ("mine").

But is she?

Her feelings, unlike his, have not been tested—and perhaps they ought to have been. Unlike P's simple "love," the woman is "loving" [him]. The unmodified use of the present progressive tense indicates that her sentiments are poten-

---

*It's this conceit that makes me think of the great metaphysical poet. However: on the grounds that a "poem should not mean / But be" (MacLeish), I argue that the playful slyness of "Good Day Sunshine" gives it a quality that an obviously virtuosic Donne poem, say, "The Flea," doesn't have. Because their conceit is almost completely hidden, the Lennon-McCartney lyrics embody the idea of the secret. And what romantic love is not a euphoric state of secrecy (from the Latin *secretus*, "separate, hidden")? Which new lovers do not feel *set apart* from the rest of the world?

tially qualified by time, and indeed may not be sentiments at all—they may be actions. She may simply be behaving in a loving way. For all of his heroism, the woman remains opaque to P and, as a consequence, opaque to us, because we see her from his perspective. P can assert only that the woman (a) feels "good," and (b) is aware that she is "looking fine"—a state of gratification that's consistent with, but not necessarily symptomatic of, her being in love with him. She may, after all, feel good merely on account of her pleasant situation—lying under a leafy tree with a knight-errant—or, for all P and we know, because her thoughts are happily else-where. Maybe she's not "his" at all. Maybe she's just being polite.

Could it be that "Good Day Sunshine," a love song fa-mous for its optimism,* is in fact a gloomy psychodrama? Is it not possible that P has taken for granted his romantic suc-cess? The story's deepest arc—barely visible, so bright is P's good mood—is also its darkest. It begins in sunlight and ends in shade.

WHEN RECORDS and record players fell into disuse, I stopped listening to our *Revolver* LP. I bought a CD of the album, I think, but I don't clearly recall, and in any case I haven't played any kind of CD in years. The family copy of

---

*Richie Unterberger, review of "Good Day Sunshine," Allmusic, 2009, http://www.allmusic.com/song/good-day-sunshine-mt0010100261.

the album, which may be a valuable 1966 copy, apparently has been lost.

A little while ago, my partner decided to buy a dinky vinyl player for the entertainment of our two-year-old daughter. The first LP we bought was *Revolver*. It became our daughter's favorite record, and her favorite song—she squawks if another comes on—is "Good Day Sunshine." When touching the ground is mentioned, she leans down and brushes a floorboard with her index finger. When lying beneath the tree is mentioned, she lies down on the floor. Otherwise she hops and slowly gyrates, which is her way of dancing and also of letting us know that she feels good.

The natural light in our New York apartment comes mostly from the west, through a pair of windows that look on Weehawken and the Hudson River. Tall, banal glass constructions have recently started to appear in the West Thirties and Forties, and before long only scraps of the river will be visible. On certain mornings, a reflection of the early sun moves across these towering hooligans. The reflection, so dazzling it can only be glanced at, produces a band of light on the floor of our apartment. Our daughter sometimes dances on this band. She is the age I was in South Africa. She may not remember this dance or this band of light, but I expect that, like so many of us, she will come to associate sunshine with the brilliant subjectivity of childhood.

SHE SAID SHE SAID

ALEC WILKINSON

I WAS THE SPECIES of moody adolescent who drove people away from me when that was the last thing I wanted, so I spent a lot of time alone. I had private enthusiasms. I liked to be in the woods by myself, I liked to sleep, I liked to swim underwater, and I liked to sit in my room and listen to music, usually repetitively, while looking at the record's cover. The first record I did this with was *The Kingston Trio at Large*, which belonged to one of my older brothers. I played it often enough that I was able finally to establish who among the three men was Dave Guard, who was Bob Shane, and who was Nick Reynolds, also who had the husky voice, who had the tenor, and who had the slightly stiff delivery. Likewise, several years later, staring at the cover of the Grateful Dead's first record, I determined who was Bob Weir, who were Captain Trips, Phil Lesh, and Bill the Drummer, and who was Pigpen. (People tend to look like their names, and when they sing they often sound like their names, too.) When *Revolver* came out, in 1966, I already knew who the individual

Beatles were—they had cunningly saturated the culture by then—but, even so, I stared at their images while I played "She Said She Said" so many times that I thought I might wear out the groove.

That year I did the same thing with "When a Man Loves a Woman" by Percy Sledge. I played "She Said She Said" because I couldn't understand it. I played "When a Man Loves a Woman" because of how beautiful it was. Of course, I couldn't understand "When a Man Loves a Woman," either. I was in eighth grade, and the emotions it concerned and the scene it described were so far beyond my knowing that I didn't even really know they existed. It was a blues song, essentially, and the blues are about things one feels most powerfully in apprehending the world's design, in maturing, that is, and I hadn't matured sufficiently yet. Adolescence, though, is almost purely a landscape of feelings, and I could believe that being in love was a lacerating, self-annihilating experience, and that a man could be in thrall to a woman.

"She Said She Said" described a mystery I could see on the horizon, vibrating like a mirage. I am the youngest by some degree of four brothers, so I was conditioned to believe and to feel that the secrets of existence were in the possession of people a few years older than I was, who were closer to the ages of the Beatles. The song's mystery seemed to lie somehow in a fracture of ordinary circumstances, as if you had taken a hammer to a mirror and cracked it in such a way that it now reflected a multiplicity of images.

I hadn't yet been given the key to the mystery, which

was LSD. I wouldn't take LSD at gunpoint now, but I used to like it a lot. I mean that I liked it when I took it; I don't mean that I took it serially or in amounts that made you forget your name or where you were. (I am thinking of a friend who took two tiny barrels of orange sunshine one night when the rest of us took one, and we had to show him the photograph on his license to persuade him that he had a name and that he wasn't an explorer from outer space. He kept appearing to have his identity almost in hand, then he would lose his grip on it, and we would have to start over again. "Francis, we're on a planet called Earth in a country called America," and so on until nearly daylight.)

I liked being in the presence of what I thought of, with no particular originality, as the wonders, and for a long time I had sensed that they were somewhere close at hand. I had seen them from the corners of my eyes, as it were—in storms, in the ocean in winter, in the stillness in the middle of the night, beneath the surface of the water, or in dreams.

The first time I took LSD was in 1969, when I was seventeen. I was at a party at the house of the older brother of one of my friends. The older people were drinking, and three or four of us teenagers were tripping. (Me, Lyle Davis, Will Colgan, and Philip Brown, an exchange student from France, if you want names.) For what I recall as a long time, I stood in front of a closet door by a washing machine. In the door's grain I saw, to my astonishment, the span of history, as if on a scroll that was unwinding. I'd bring people to stand in front of the door with me, and I'd point out Jesus, and

Charlemagne, and soldiers with lances riding elephants, and I'd say, "See?!"

As a young child, I was susceptible to something I think of as overloaded time, which probably is not unusual and was signified by a feeling that a gear had slipped and left me where I was, while the world continued a degree ahead of me. Once the state was upon me, the background withdrew, and my attention was overtaken by a scene's particular elements. A shaft of sunlight coming through the curtain in my parents' living room might seem to swirl with particles, which later, I realized, were dust, but when I was three and four they seemed like the texture of air itself. I thought I could see what air is made of. If I moved, the particles formed new patterns—it was like turning the end of a kaleidoscope. Or I might awake from a dream but the dream would continue as a projection on a wall. If someone came between me and the wall, I saw the image projected on him or her, like a light show in a nightclub. I was probably having a mild seizure of some kind, but while the state was upon me, I had the feeling that time was a series of pieces that fit together like joints in furniture, and every now and then one encountered the seams, rather than having time be like, say, a river, or a wheel that turned in an orderly way.

Very few songs influenced by a drug reproduce the sensation of taking the drug, but "She Said She Said" comes close. It's a solemn song and seems to coil snakelike in on itself. Before *Rubber Soul* and *Revolver*, most Beatles songs had been intended to reach the broadest audience by dramatizing feelings everyone has had, but "She Said She Said" is a private matter, which appealed to me—overloaded time being a state of mind congenial to self-consciousness. The other acid song on the record, "Tomorrow Never Knows," is inclusive, asking the listener to submit to the riverine current of consciousness. Join me, it says. "She Said She Said" is a witness song. A piece of theater. You're listening to an argument, a dialectic. "I know what it's like," one character says. "No, no, no, you're wrong," the other says. Another dichotomy it contains is one between Harrison's shiny, chiming guitar lines, which seem to thread the song together, and Starr's drumming, which seems constantly to threaten a collapse. "She Said She Said" and "Tomorrow Never Knows" were the farthest ahead of the culture the Beatles ever got. A lot of people think "A Day in the Life" is, but that song's effect depends mainly on the song cycle–like arrangement of material. It's a Lennon song and a McCartney song stitched together by George Martin by means of effects from classical and avant-garde music. "She Said She Said" describes circumstances novel to Western awareness and has no obvious antecedent or reference. It is a conversation undertaken by means of access to a form of consciousness induced by a drug, which was known then only to a small number of practitioners.

I would listen over and over to the song while looking at the cover. Something was different about the musicians. They had always looked out at the world, and now they were looking at one another. They wore dark glasses and were photographed in what appeared to be darkness. The darkness didn't seem manipulated so as to be sinister—their expressions were still cheerful—but it indicated an inversion of the ordinary. It had a glamour, as did everything they did. Their appeal was so broad that it forced the Rolling Stones to seek their identity sometimes in the shadow of it or in straightforward imitation, as with their own psychedelic album, but mostly in contrast to it. The Stones' idea—to inhabit the modes and gestures of black American music—was a smaller idea attractively enacted.

I hadn't felt the things that the narrator was singing about, and I wasn't sure what they were. They seemed forbidding. Were they actual? What did it mean to feel like you'd never been born? Adolescents are, I think, mainly literal-minded. They assume, when they are being instructed by example or inference, that language corresponds fairly directly to experience. They respond to fancy writing, for its suggestion of subversiveness, but the response has something of the quality of being a badge—*I'm not afraid of this*. By carrying this book with me, I have a certain command of it. Baudelaire, for example, and *The Flowers of Evil*, which was popular among adolescents in my day and may still be. The books became causes. They established your identity, like a tattoo. They might carry the implication *My book is scarier than yours, or more high-minded*. How would it feel to have never been born? How could another person make you feel that way? It was as if the walls had to come down to accommodate such a point of view. Or as if the walls could be seen through.

In the middle of the song, there is a passage of three-quarter time, the point where Lennon sings about how everything was fine when he was a boy, and the effect is as if he has taken a breath to recover himself.

There is no stagecraft, as in "Tomorrow Never Knows," the other futuristic song. There are no crying birds in the background, only two guitars, a bass, drums, and a droning organ. They could have played this song live, and I wish they had.

The first time John Lennon took LSD, it was given to him surreptitiously, at a dinner party in London at his dentist's house, in 1966. Lennon's wife, Cynthia, was there, and so were George Harrison and Pattie Boyd, his girlfriend who became his wife. After the dentist told them what they had taken—Lennon thought he had put it in their coffee—he said they shouldn't leave, which led Lennon and Harrison to think that he was planning an orgy. They got in Harrison's car instead and drove to a nightclub called the Ad Lib. The club was on an upper floor, and they thought that the elevator, which had a red light, was on fire. A singer Lennon knew asked if he could sit next to him and Lennon said, "Only if you don't talk," since Lennon couldn't think clearly.

Eventually Harrison drove them to his house. He went about ten miles an hour, but Lennon thought it felt like a thousand. Harrison and Boyd went to bed. Lennon stayed up and made some drawings, which he later gave to Ringo.

Harrison's house had a high wall around it. Lennon thought that the house was a submarine and that it had risen up above the wall, and he was steering it.

The second time Lennon took LSD was in Los Angeles at the end of the Beatles' last tour of America. Their manager, Brian Epstein, had rented a house for a week for them to recover. Once the address got out, they were more or less captives, since so many people showed up that the police had to defend the place.

Among the people who visited the house were the Byrds and Peter Fonda, who made the song's remark about being dead. Fonda has said that he made it while trying to comfort Harrison, who thought he was dying. As a boy, Fonda had accidentally shot himself. On the operating table his heart stopped three times. Lennon said that Fonda kept showing the scar and whispering, "I know what it's like to be dead." "We were saying, 'For Christ's sake, shut up. We don't care, we don't want to know.'" In Lennon's first versions of the song, he sings, "He said."

Somewhere in the psyche is everything we can imagine. Cities we have never visited, characters, landscapes, circumstances that will appear in dreams, all brought into being by some agency we don't fully understand and can't summon easily in waking life. "She Said She Said" seemed to me, alone in my room, like a bulletin from the other side of the fence (even though I didn't yet know there was a fence), and it still does.

I no more understood these things than I understand

now the mysteries of deep old age, which I hope to live long enough to experience. I was simply taken in by the music. I followed Lennon's voice like a Scheherazade story. The rapturous music made me feel powerful, and since it is essentially a solitary song, it enforced my isolation, which had a sweetness to it that loneliness in adult life does not.

I am no longer that boy. Certainly some elements of our natures survive, are even indestructible, perhaps, but since childhood I have had so many experiences, good and bad—so many disappointments, and, I hesitate to call them successes—nevertheless experiences that sustain me, that I can't feel myself anything except different. Jung somewhere observes that lives often collapse in cycles of seven years, a notion derived, I think, from an alchemical principle. What he means are assumptions about the self. The task is to put them back together in a new way. The novelist Reynolds Price, who became confined to a wheelchair at the age of fifty when radiation treatments for cancer eroded his spine, said to himself one morning, "Reynolds Price is dead. Who are you going to be now?"

The borderline in our memories with the past, and not even the very faraway past, is the territory where we begin groping for facts and meaning. Certain things return naturally, aggressively, even. Others prefer the shadows or even the darkness. It is no observation of my own that the past is the territory of lies. The person I was is lost and can't be recovered. I can only re-create him, a gloomy adolescent, alone in his room, holding a record cover, listening to the mystery.

STRAWBERRY FIELDS FOREVER / PENNY LANE

ADAM GOPNIK

I HAVE ALWAYS THOUGHT IT a shame that "Penny Lane" and "Strawberry Fields," the two finest songs from the Beatles sessions that produced *Sgt. Pepper's Lonely Hearts Club Band*, could not, according to the brutal commercial rules of the period, be placed on the album after having first appeared as a 45. (Remember those? Remember albums?) Yet spending a morning finding a place for them amid the familiar tracks proves much harder than one might have imagined. The rule of Beatles album composition was that the "closer" on an album side should be, so to speak, unanswerable, conclusive. "Strawberry Fields" could certainly sit on the end of side one, in place of "Mr. Kite," and achieve that, rather like "I Want You" on *Abbey Road*. But then again it might have been too sepulchral, too conclusive, too far out of the fairground fantasy world of the record, broken properly only once by "A Day in the Life" on the end of side two.

And if "Penny Lane" is to open side two, well, it seems too complete a work to open anything. It needs to be the end of something, too. (One feels a similar uneasiness trying to fit "Hey Jude" onto the White Album; it's too big to be contained by other songs. And so, in its more miniature scale, is "Penny Lane".)

No, the double-A-sided single belongs as a small masterpiece alongside the bigger one—and, perhaps, in a way, an even bigger masterpiece than the larger record; a perfect expression of the Beatles' art at the high point of their artistry, at the pivotal moment when they turned from pop entertainment to invent a new form of their own—genuinely artful in its indifference to conventional expectations, genuinely pop in its ability to communicate immediate emotion immediately. In this case, the emotion communicated was a simple one, the classic Wordsworthian emotion, a longing for childhood places and peace in the midst of the confusions of adulthood. With my chin only slightly out and leading, I'd even argue, or anyway assert, that this simple single was the most significant work of art produced in the 1960s, the one that articulated the era's hopes for a crossover of pop art and high intricacy, and that summed up, in poignant poetic form, the decade's surprising desire, which was not for revolution, but instead for renewed innocence. For a little while anyway, such music suggested that anything was possible, and made what was possible seem what was most humane.

The story of how the two songs came to be recorded is

familiar—or familiar to Beatles fans, anyway, but, fifty-plus years on, still might be briefly retold. Both were recorded at the very beginning of what became the *Sgt. Pepper* sessions, in December of 1966, and then in the first month of 1967. John had written "Strawberry Fields" while shooting the Richard Lester movie *How I Won the War* the previous summer in Spain. "Penny Lane" had emerged under Paul's hand from the earlier drafts of the cowritten "In My Life," where the Liverpool shopping street was at first to have been featured, too. Both songs took as their subjects, against the grain of pop music, not love or unrequited love or infatuation or jealousy, but childhood memory. (Strawberry Field was the name of the Salvation Army garden where the young John went often for holiday fetes.)

Against the grain, perhaps, but not entirely without precedent. The strain of English nostalgia was a powerful and often too-overlooked element in the British Invasion. Just as British kids of the Beatles generation had been in love with the simple sounds of American places—"Texas!" "Miami!" ("Chicago" had worked the same magic for the Brecht-Weill generation)—American kids responded to the new exoticism of the English. The Kinks, above all, with songs like "A Well Respected Man," but also the Hollies with "Bus Stop"—umbrella fetishism being a very English preoccupation—and even the Stones with "Lady Jane" had all mined a vein of Englishness that was utterly transfixing to an American audience. And let us not shame or amnesia away Herman's Hermits, who had vied with the Stones'

"Satisfaction" for the number one record in America in the summer of 1966 with the hyper-English "I'm Henry VIII, I Am." This was a vein, in fact, that the Kinks in particular would go on to exploit beautifully, producing both their *Village Green Preservation Society* the next year, and then their masterpiece, *Arthur, or the Decline and Fall of the British Empire*, in 1969, the latter with its still unsurpassed "Victoria," Ray Davies's Larkinian anthem of Little England longing for the lost past. It's a vein of national nostalgia that never entirely passed, informing the work of the great songwriter Martin Newell, and in another way, that of his sometime collaborator, Andy Partridge of XTC (cf. the 1989 "Mayor of Simpleton").

So the idea of England was to sixties pop what the idea of Japan had been to French Impressionism—the idealized other place, at once quaint and vivid. (This idea would blossom in the beautiful Beatles-related though not supervised *Yellow Submarine*, where the imaginary Pepperland is a lost Arcadian England.) It is difficult for Kids Today to quite grasp how exotic and appealing even the smoky cold gray and white England of *A Hard Day's Night* looked to American contemporaries. The things that were dowdy and sometimes still war-ruined looked merely artisanal and charming: the train compartments with their sliding doors, the run-down docks and pubs, the gray, wet London air. Both sides of the single draw on this vein of feeling—as a sequence of images in "Penny Lane," as a mood of feeling in "Strawberry Fields."

The argument in "Strawberry Fields" is that there was a

better-lost place somewhere in the singer's past, which seems achingly desirable in the midst of his current confusion. The music makes that longing palpable, but it also, in the richness of its color and the surprise of its orchestration, makes it present in an arresting new way that even "In My Life" could not quite achieve. We can follow the musical evolution of "Strawberry Fields" from first demo to finished product, perhaps better than we can that of any other Beatle song, thanks to the many preserved versions; some, though only some, were included on the second volume of the *Anthology* series. (The rest can easily be found on YouTube.) One hears John struggling with his own inventions. On one of the first demos, the tight, four-beat strum pattern imitates that of "Yesterday"; then he tries fingerpicking his way through the song, only to announce, "It doesn't work like that." He ends with a more familiar, Lennonesque rhythmic up-and-down stroke. "Let me take you back . . ." he sings, rather than "down." The chord pattern is unique in a Beatles song, filled with what were, for rock, still exotic chords—major fifths and sevenths—arrived at empirically on the guitar.

Musically, though, the song only comes entirely to life when Paul adds the Mellotron part to the first electric takes, accompanied also by George's slide guitar—not yet a Harrison signature, though beautifully played here, with Paul's discovery of the perfect supporting figure acting as a lovely instance of the writing duo's quieter form of support for each other. It is arguable that John never quite matched the level of childlike pathos in the finished recording, with his voice heavily treated, that he found in those early demos. (A highlight of the Beatles reunion tour, which economic pressure would doubtless have dictated in the 1990s, had John lived, would have been his acoustic version of the song.) Yet take four, the first electric recording, has a near-perfect Lennon vocal, and may be the most pleasing of all the many takes, even if it lacks the richness and audacity of the final track. Confusingly, it has a full bass and Mellotron part, so presumably is a composite, with Paul playing both.

As every fan knows, this first version was then replaced by a faster, orchestral version with a George Martin score, which was then also rejected, with John insisting on melding together the first half of the electric version with the second half of the orchestral one—a feat achieved only with some electronic prestidigitation by Martin and the engineer, Geoff Emerick. Martin's arrangement is in itself like nothing else in pop music—biting cellos and Purcell trumpets— but John's instinct was perfect; on its own the orchestral version sounds too strange and aggressive. The final version, melding the dreamy plangency of the slide guitar and Mellotron version with the incisive bite of the orchestral one, one sliding seamlessly into the other, is what makes the masterpiece. If something of freshness and childlike emotion is lost along the way, the collage effect and the funhouse-like sense of surprise make up for it. The final emotional spell it casts is less nostalgic and longing than present-tense and enunciated—Strawberry Fields becomes not the place we go back to but the place we go down to. It's available—through psychedelics most obviously, through mind transformations of all kinds implicitly.

"Penny Lane" has a more shadowy production history. We read of Paul making a composite keyboard track, very much under the spell of Brian Wilson's *Pet Sounds* sound, where woodwinds and keyboards, flutes and piano, together make up a single composite tone, at once expansively breathy and percussively clean. The piano carries the movement of the song in a way that it did on earlier songs with a similarly strong classical, or even music hall, underpinning—"For No One" and "Good Day Sunshine" both come to mind. The song's chord sequence is still a thing of wonder—almost without precedent in the Beatles' own work, and still without many musical offspring. (Where, for instance, the "Let It Be" chord children are innumerable.) The mid-key switch from major to minor, heard first on the lyric "portrait of the Queen"—not major to relative minor, a favorite device of Richard Rodgers, Paul's only peer in leap-in-the-dark melody making, but from the tonic major to its own minor, B to B minor—is one Paul played with many times in this period, most memorably in "The Fool on the Hill," where the main strain is in sweet C major and the refrain is in poignant C minor. In this case, though, the tonic chord of B, an unusual key in pop music, first goes to the VI, a flat minor, only then to move back to B minor, a startling shift. (The tonality of the song is micro-adjusted electronically, so it is not in true concert pitch, a thing of fiendish confusion to generations of amateur guitarists.) But where the shift from major to minor registers in "The Fool on the Hill" as a clear change in purpose, from affirmation to melancholy, here it is part of a more general mood making, somehow conveying the mixed emotional and literal weather of the song—rainy days and sunny measures, blue skies interrupted by short afternoon showers; exactly the world that the song's lyric celebrates.

The carpentry of the track is astonishing, with the many parts—keyboard, wind, bass—all coming together in one glorious thump. The most famous overdub in Beatles music replaced a decent but mildly corny cor anglais part with David Mason's piccolo trumpet, which Paul had heard on a BBC broadcast of the Bach Second Brandenburg. (It is a sign of how healthy the middlebrow culture of the period was that Bach's Brandenburgs were played on television.) Mason proudly insists in subsequent interviews that the extremely difficult high-trumpet part—composed, it seems, by Paul on piano with George Martin's transcription—"made" the record. It didn't do that, but it decorated a beautifully made thing perfectly.

"Penny Lane" is explicitly longing and nostalgic, where "Strawberry Fields" is implicitly so. The singer catalogs the sights of the far-off future and the past: he is sitting now under blue suburban skies—presumably Paul had in mind John's incongruous suburban house in the "Banker Belt," where they wrote together so often—and meanwhile, back in Penny Lane, things go on. We are to take this surely, to be both the northern present and the poetic past: Penny Lane is still thriving and Liverpool goes on intact—this happened in a still-existing place—but, the singer insists, it happened best when I was younger and free to be an anonymous part of the scene. As "down" functions in "Strawberry Fields" to lead us not only to childhood memory but to their retaking today, "back" in "Penny Lane" has an implicit double meaning, too: all this life and liveliness is going on now on Penny Lane, but I recall it from a time now lost to me. It's safe, back up in Liverpool; it's lost, back in my past—just as it's "down" in Strawberry Fields, not "back" in it, since everybody has a Strawberry Fields somewhere down in their soul.

At the most straightforward level, both songs are a reminder that the Liverpool the Beatles grew up in was still an essentially healthy city, where working-class kids had access to decent housing—George could recall the joy of their first council house—and decent education, so that Paul still talks of the English masters who brought him to poetry and Shakespeare, while his *Liverpool Oratorio* takes the motto of the Liverpool Institute, where he and George went to school—"Not for ourselves but for the whole world were we born"—with complete seriousness.

And yet the specificity of the time and place recalled makes the afterlife of both songs interestingly limited. They are classics without quite being standards. The number of covers of either one is limited, considering they were Beatles number ones; they are so intently made, they don't invite *re*making. The psychedelic sound with which they were (falsely) associated was short-lived. The possibilities of this layered, collage-like production bloomed and then largely went to seed after. (Had Brian Wilson's *Smile* survived its contact with the Beatles' musicality, it might have gone somewhere, though *Smile* is adulterated even in its later complete form by a tad too much whimsicality. "Vegetables," indeed.) The Stones took the sound to a stoned cul-de-sac in *Their Satanic Majesties Request* and then had to reinvigorate themselves with Mick Taylor's blues guitar. To take one instance of a thousand, the arrangements on James Taylor's first Beatles-produced record try to capture the same Baroque-pop mood, but JT needed to clean out that stable, too, in order to arrive at the cleaner, purer sound of *Sweet Baby James*. Although the distinctive cellos and acid horns and flutes appeared again when an artist wanted to evoke the earlier period—as in Prince's "Raspberry Beret"—it is, then, a self-conscious evocation of the Beatles' high-water mark rather than an extension of its own. The single stands apart, a perfect accomplishment.

"Strawberry Fields" is remembered, most poignantly, as a patch of Central Park named after John, who lived nearby. But perhaps the finest moment in the life of the double-A-sided single came more than forty years later, when Elvis Costello sang "Penny Lane" beautifully with that mature Costello vibrato, at the White House as McCartney was being honored by President Obama. "Music is often an 'us against them' proposition," he said—but this song wasn't, and he recalled hearing it for the first time on the radio: "It was named after a place my mother comes from, and when we heard this thing of wonder and beauty—myself as a young man, my dad, my mam, and the cat—all stood up and took notice." Someone said, with teasing hyperbole, that the world had not been as united since the Congress of Vienna as it was the week *Sgt. Pepper* came out. But there was a high truth to it, too.

By report, the trumpet solo in the song was to be played at the White House on the keyboard, as it is in McCartney's concert tours, but the Marine trumpeter in the president's personal band took it for granted that he could play it, and he did, beautifully. He knew it—as so many of us do these songs—by heart.

A DAY IN THE LIFE

NICHOLAS DAWIDOFF

WHO EVER LOVED POP MUSIC who loved not at first sight? I first heard the Beatles as a little kid, around 1970, at a babysitter's home, an experience so instantly exhilarating that I still think of it every time I walk past that house in a "George Washington Slept Here" sort of way. Back at my own house, it turned out those George Washingtons slept here, there, and everywhere. When I told my mother what I'd heard, she, who liked Mozart and CBS news on the radio, went to her record shelf and produced a copy of *Rubber Soul*. It was the only rock album in her collection. I was astonished. "You like the Beatles?!" I said. She replied, "Who wouldn't like something that beautiful?"

From friends ten years older, I know what it was like to experience the Beatles' music in real time. Performers released fewer albums then, they were usually made quickly, and even the best had the feeling of several good singles packaged together (with filler). Then came *Rubber Soul* and *Revolver*. Those albums sounded so unique that people wondered, *was something wrong with their stereo?* Each was an ensemble suite of original songs that had striking musical expression and depth of personal meaning—adult expression in what had been music for kids. For a listener, it was great art encountered unmediated, and one result was an elevating general regard for four-minute songs—although nobody quite yet said the Beatles' music (or rock music) was art.

After *Rubber Soul* and *Revolver,* in the long record-breaking summer heat of 1967, had come something new again. Paul McCartney envisioned *Sgt. Pepper's Lonely Hearts Club Band* as a conceptual means of the band looking back on younger versions of themselves, and the thirteen songs have internal unity that makes the whole seem like the point. Inspired by Brian Wilson's obsessive labor on the Beach Boys' epic *Pet Sounds,* the *Sgt. Pepper* studio sessions were weeks of ideas tried, ideas rejected, and things attempted anew. Part of *Sgt. Pepper*'s achievement is that it represented what popular music could aspire to. Because the Beatles took their careful time with it, *Sgt. Pepper* took over its time.

Back in the 1940s, when Bob Wills and His Texas Playboys released a new song, it could be heard simultaneously all across West Texas and Oklahoma on virtually every dryland farm. *Sgt. Pepper* was that kind of regional experience gone cross-country. In June and July 1967, the American response was such that just about anywhere a person went, there was *Sgt. Pepper*—pouring out of cars, apartment windows, stores, and building lobbies—the entire album, all day long. It wasn't just that people liked it; to some of them there was also the intense satisfaction of adjudicating its significance. Instead of a teacher telling you about Picasso or *The Great Gatsby*, you could listen and assess for yourself, and so you became the mediator.

In my life, the Beatles were never a passion like bands of my own youth, such as Talking Heads and Elvis Costello and the Attractions, that I heard in their moment and blindly fell for; the Beatles were a desire more lovely and more temperate—and one completely mediated. By the time I was of fanly age, in the late 1970s and early 1980s, the Beatles were yesterday, a thing of *Will there ever be a reunion?* speculations, tribute bands, and Broadway revues. Teenagers want music of their own to be close to, something that individuates and expresses their moment. When a kid named Arnold brought Stevie Wonder's *Songs in the Key of Life* to school, the way he carried the double album, outside his textbooks like a coat of arms, said this meant so much it was him. No one I grew up with listened to Beatles records.

Yet they remained omnipresent. Even before classic rock existed, the songs were always all around you. You learned them from the radio, mismatched, helter-skelter, out of release order, such sturdy members of the canon that even now there are Beatle Blocks, Breakfasts with the Beatles, the endless caller requests. In the 1970s, everybody still had a favorite Beatle. If yours was John, there he was, bantering on talk shows and *Monday Night Football*. Paul wrote "Silly Love Songs." *The Spy Who Loved Me* married Ringo. George we heard less and less about until several years after "Layla" when his wife became Clapton's, whereupon we heard a bit too much. Every kind of everybody—starting with Otis, Stevie, Al, Judy, and Bowie—seemed to cover them. Every other year when the Stones put out another record, they were second-best all over again.

It's commonplace for rock songs to achieve lifelong associative resonance with a strong personal experience. If the radio plays Pure Prairie League's "Amie," I am back in a stuffy college dorm room on a winter afternoon where a roommate is singing it by way of mocking me about my first big romantic disappointment. That he could see me in my predicament with such ease said it was common, said I was inexperienced, and said that my lack of experience had made me unattractive to her and now also vulnerable to him. R.E.M.'s "Driver 8" brings me again into the sunny New York apartment where I slept on a friend's couch while saving up enough deposit money to rent my first room—most things still a ways away, but life opening up, everything on the point of beginning. Anxious in my early twenties, I shared an office with a man in his thirties named Merrell, who fundamentally didn't worry about what other people thought of him, though he became indignant if you didn't sufficiently appreciate the Kinks' "Waterloo Sunset." The sudden clarity of hearing what Bruce Springsteen was singing about in a song I'd known for years, "Independence Day," is all I remember of the week right after my father's death.

Beatles songs were, of course, soundtracks to similarly

charged days in the lives of millions of people like me, but such was the Beatles' musical intelligence that by my time it was clear their brief songs had uncommon feeling. The Beatles spoke to people at all sentient stages of life, expressed the universality of emotion across generations. It wasn't just that everyone wants to hold hands. At first the idea of it, like the song itself, can seem insipid—right up until you suddenly experience the urge yourself, whereupon life, as with John and Paul's switchback vocals, becomes far more complicated. *Let It Be* was often played at the saddest occasions, strengthening the impression that Beatles songs were, like quotations from Shakespeare, the musical means of expressing enduring consequence. That they were the standard for pop gravitas was confirmed for me when I attended a senior prom at someone else's high school, a dance named "The Long and Winding Road." That was a song we all knew, never chose to listen to, but understood to be worthy of the big occasion.

With all the good songs out there by all the good bands through all the years, it's an amazing thing that people keep asking for and returning to so many of the Beatles' songs. Just last night I heard "Paperback Writer." My own primary criterion for my favorite rock songs is simply how many repeated listenings they can sustain. Do I crave them across time? When I do it's because even in the familiarity there is still mystery and surprise. Since there are so many Beatles songs to choose from, it becomes possible to experience the essential pop music self-delusion with them, that something so massively well-known could still be personal to you.

Many, many people across many generations share my favorite things: "West End Blues" and "I'm So Lonesome I Could Cry," *The Third Man* and *The Sting*, Pieter Bruegel the Elder's paintings and Robert Frank's photographs, *My Ántonia* and *The Life of Johnson*, "A Change Is Gonna Come" and "Something So Right." It's really in combination with the others, involuntarily curated by me, that makes my favorite Beatles song, "A Day in the Life," mine.

Like most people of unusual talent, the Beatles grounded stellar inspiration in hard work. They made "A Day in the Life" as they made many of the songs on *Sgt. Pepper*, like masons. It's received wisdom that *Sgt. Pepper* is one of rock's greatest albums, but I don't consider it even the best Beatles album. There's the much-noted abundance of interesting experiment, but that sum falls far short of *Rubber Soul*'s and *Revolver*'s (and the White Album's) wholes. It's this great, great song, rather than the album, that is the epitome of their master building, of fitting stone upon stone, each section troweled together with such ingenuity and care that upon completion the whole thing feels seamless, a structure not built at all, but a whole that simply was. There's so much going on here that Trilling-at-the-page close-reading is very possible. But doing so, I fear, may take the fun out of it for me. Love is, after all, no longer love when it too much contemplates altering what it finds. I don't want to reduce all the little epiphanies with scrutiny. Liking songs is risky. They are aural fireflies, and you can get too close and lose them. If "A Day in the Life" is about anything, it speaks to the way the daily unfolding of worldly events touches the private fragilities of ordinary people. It's *Ulysses* in a pop song, the typical day made unforgettable.

I've never considered "A Day in the Life" a song to sing as are "Eleanor Rigby" (ideal for both car and karaoke), "Hey Jude" (written to soothe John Lennon's young son and undefeated at children's bedtime), or "In My Life" (a perennial at weddings and funerals and, I can't help mentioning, rock's analog to Sonnet 116). "A Day in the Life" isn't guided by a melody as those songs are. It's an elaborate production, filled with sophisticated George Martin and Geoff Emerick musical trickery (distortion, echo, dubbing, reverb). An orchestra appears, there are the famous handoffs from one singer's voice to another, John's worldly reflections transitioning to Paul's sketch of domestic memoir, and then back again, before orchestral cataclysm and a final resting place.

The song has so much happening that when I casually listen I feel the accumulated effect, but if I attempt to get at it more artfully, really adduce what's going on, I always fail. I once spent an afternoon with Paul Simon as he took me through one of his new songs. He explained every sound, why everything was, and yet afterward, on my own, I fell back. I am incapable of following the lyrics in counterpoint with the onrush of musical ideas, can hear only in mono. I get distracted by how compelling and pleasing one thing is, and everything else sails calmly on without me. I am often struck in this way by Ringo's quietly self-possessed drumming. Usually I have no insight into drummers, can never hear all the ecstasy others do in the sticks of Bonham or Moon, Roach or Krupa. Instruments suggest aspects of the human singing voice, but rarely does that truth occur to me because of a drummer. Yet it does here with Ringo. The other Beatles pressed him to take the instrumental lead in this song, and to use his toms. Then someone had the idea of wrapping the drum microphones in towels to muffle his fills. I like that Ringo's way of asserting himself involves restraint.

Something else in "A Day in the Life" that catches me in the back of the knees time after time is John's singing. Bob Spitz writes that Lennon's model here was Elvis performing "Heartbreak Hotel," but John's vocal, climbing to falsetto through the dreamy tape-echo distortions, compares with nobody else I have ever heard. That rising reedy quaver is the very sound of something unprotected and fleeting. The simplest phrases, the way he says "House of Lords," the way he lingers over the famous "Ahhhh" get me so moved I believe I can hear countries and oceans in his voice, both the Ireland and the Liverpool, and maybe the whole diaspora in between. When we speak of a vocalist's range, typically we are talking about how low and high they can go. With Lennon, the range had to do with depth; his voice seems to travel further and further inward. Lennon's Groucho Marx eyebrows and caustic wit make it easy to remember him mugging it up for the people. On me, his voice falls so hard that everything else, including a full-steam blast of horns, disappears. But that's how days are, isn't it? In the infinity of interaction and event, you yourself notice a grain of sound.

Songs and albums exert fundamentally different listening experiences. My favorite rock album, the Rolling Stones' *Exile on Main St.*, contains none of my favorite rock songs. I have two kinds of favorite rock songs. There are the songs that, after I get to know them, I like best to encounter unexpectedly. Bill Withers's "Lean on Me," Warren Zevon's "Werewolves of London," Janis Joplin's "Piece of My Heart," Johnny Nash's "I Can See Clearly Now," and Dire Straits' "Sultans of Swing" are once-in-a-while-caught-on-the-radio faves. When I fall hard for a song, for a while it becomes a compulsion, the only song there is, and I listen over and over and over. This has happened with Queen's "Bohemian Rhapsody" (at age thirteen), Jimmy Cliff's "The Harder They Come," Randy Newman's "Baltimore," Talking Heads' "Once in a Lifetime," Lucinda Williams's "Right in Time," Counting Crows' "Mr. Jones," Freedy Johnston's "Bad Reputation," Gnarls Barkley's "Crazy," Etta James's "Sugar on the Floor," and right now, the War on Drugs' "Under the Pressure." Just listing all these songs brings me such pleasure that I have to resist going back (a fourth time) and adding more. In only a few cases has this sort of obsessive period of needing to hear it happened more than once with the same song. (The Clash's "London Calling" and Bob Dylan's "Tangled Up in Blue" are two of these.)

So here's what I can report after the latest of the many hours I've spent listening again and again to "A Day in the Life." Instead of a propulsive "Can't Buy Me Love" up-tempo, this has a moodier start, appropriate for a song of portent.

The early piano, guitar, and maracas meet John's voice in humming tremors of sound. John was a whatever-gets-you-through-the-night kind of guy, the sort of person who'd respond to headline news in the paper of a young man dying in a car wreck with a laugh and some distancing irony—in this case he remarks, "Oh, boy!" *Oh, boy* is one of those phrases so strongly associated with another musician—Buddy Holly—that I can't hear it without thinking of him and his song "Oh, Boy!" As it happens, the Beatles were such fans of Holly and his band, the Crickets, that they named their band in both crawly-thing and double entendre homage to his. Early in his music career, Lennon had been self-conscious about being a kid who wore glasses, lived in a semi-detached, and wanted to make rock and roll. That Holly had seen the world through black suburban frames was vastly reassuring to him. Lennon told the journalist Jim Dawson that he knew how to play all of Holly's songs, and thought so much about them that "what he did with three chords made a songwriter out of me." Truly creative people put more into what they make than even they are sometimes aware. I don't know if John Lennon was embedding a Holly reference in "A Day in the Life," but the tragic event in the song does sort of mirror young Holly's death in a plane crash, which had been front-page news itself eight years before. What Lennon most prized about Holly was his ability to sing while also playing music; he didn't just wield an instrument for effect. "A Day in the Life" is an apotheosis of his soaring musical ambition.

What exactly is happening? In the best rock songs, you can *almost* see it. When Paul told me a girl was just seventeen and I knew what he meant, in fact I didn't know what he meant, which was the point. "Mystery Train" is a perfect rock title because, well, what is that? "A Day in the Life" is filled with a collage of images in enticing half focus. Lennon, the crowd, you, and I are all voyeurs, transfixed by something horrible, the newsworthy death. Everybody recognizes the victim but nobody knows exactly who he is. Was he a politician? When Lennon mentions the House of Lords, I always think of the Profumo scandal, that early-sixties period when politics began to merge with mass-media-driven celebrity in a way that sharply undermined popular assumptions about Great Men. Whose day in the life is it, anyway? The crowd's life or simply the singer's? And is it still your life if your crucial experiences are received secondhand, from articles and cameras? Was Lennon himself so famous now that he was forced to live life from the passive privacy of an easy chair?

That's how he was writing, beachcombing inspiration from headlines and news briefs in the January 17 *Daily Mail*, which he had open at his piano (for this song); from a circus poster hanging in his home ("Being for the Benefit of Mr. Kite"); from a cereal advertisement ("Good Morning Good Morning"); from his child's drawing ("Lucy in the Sky with Diamonds"); and soon from a hobby magazine headline ("Happiness Is a Warm Gun"). In the newspaper, the young man who dies was an acquaintance of the Beatles, a

Guinness beer company heir named Tara Browne, who crashed his Lotus sports car at high speed. Lennon turns him into the half-recognizable, presumably upper-class man who has it made and then throws it all away. What does it say that one crowd is transfixed by a privileged stranger's grisly demise, but another crowd rejects a movie involving the achievement of a generation, the World War won? Only the moviegoer is willing to go back there, and only because he read the book.

You want to go back there and you don't. A perilous, self-destructive time is being described, along with emptiness adrift, the desire for substance, something to hold on to. Lennon might be the enemy of nostalgia, but he understands its appeal. There's no single feeling. Lennon didn't like his voice, but the rest of us did because, as is true in this song, and in others like "I'm So Tired," it seemed like several voices at once—intimate, seductive, raspy, bemused, distanced, and pissed off. Achieving that much emotional overlap in sound and substance within such a concentrated amount of space is thrilling.

If "In My Life" was Lennon's autobiographical look back on the time before he joined the Beatles, "A Day in the Life" seems to be how he experienced the quotidian as a Beatle. His conversation on talk shows and in magazine interviews revealed close engagement with current events—unsurprising, as he's commonly remembered as an artist who hoped to effectuate change; remembered for the radical interludes when he took on sex, love, and the Vietnam War; remembered as the working-class hero who worried Nixon. But in this song he seems most at home as an observer, in retreat at the piano, looking out at the busy world from a housebound distance, as a creative writer would, rather than as an activist-journalist. Some of Lennon's songwriting contemporaries were lifting their lyrics from old blues or from overheard conversations in bars. That Lennon extracted his details from the daily throng of public images and then transposed them as, say, Philip Larkin did with his own everyday experiences means the song is his life. He had such a quick intelligence, was so restlessly curious. Everything interested him, and that's why the random information in this song feels true to him as a man who took the most pleasure from mining the ephemeral day-to-day and refashioning it into permanence as songs. As Lennon eventually admitted, his activism came from guilt and obligation. He understood politics, but his outlook was artistic. I can't think of a popular song that references more different forms of art—photography, film, literature, architecture. In that respect, "A Day in the Life" is autobiography as interior still life, a person selecting representative images to show you how he experiences the world.

And then, halfway through, he pauses and, in the celebrated phrase, he wants to turn someone else on.

In the sixties, that phrase signaled Dr. Timothy Leary and LSD, especially to the BBC, which banned the song because of the drug reference. But with Lennon, who reveled in puns, wordplay, verbal sleight of hand, you could never be so literal. Maybe it's because I know Lennon was always ahead

of his time, but I hear the impulse to use the phrase the way
we do now, as an omnibus for stimulation—to turn you on
to a book or film, to turn you on sexually, or simply to get
you going. (The phrase "blew his mind" is similarly ambiguous, multivalent.) It interests me in all respects that the line,
which John called "a beautiful little lick," was actually
Paul's, that it made Paul think of John, and that, in the song,
John sings it to introduce his collaborator, Paul. "Now and
then we really turn each other on with a bit of song," John
said much later, thinking back to the moment.

All my life I've heard variously that John was the artist
and Paul something less, that Paul broke up the band with
his domineering self-importance, that, in fact, Paul was way
deeper and darker than people (and John) gave him credit
for, that it was all Yoko's fault, and so on and on and on. In
the end, it seems that everybody began missing them at the
split, immediately required a villain, and some still do. Even
now, with two of them gone, there are plenty of people still
lamenting the breakup as though it is fresh and reversible.

The point is, the whole was so much more than the sum
of the four independent parts. How could it not have been?
And how rare that they all stuck it out as four for so long.
The history of rock is full of bands with one shimmering
frontman and secondary players. Only the Beatles had two
equal and versatile musicians who, beyond their singing,
writing, and playing, were also magnetically handsome,
photogenic, intelligent, and charming. The nature of such
artists is to go it alone at the lead. "A Day in the Life" makes

me see how close John and Paul were, how well they understood and appreciated each other as artists, how their songs
came from an oscillating process of writerly separation and
then joining together, how skillful they were, a little universe of invention—all those vivid images and internal
rhymes turned out as casually as woodworkers with a lathe.
In this respect, it's "A Day in the Life" of a songwriting team,
working alone, coming together by delivering parts to each
other's houses, helping, suggesting, competing, vitiating,
and then improving, pushing each other even as they offer
their own view of things. Which is exactly how they both
described the writing of "A Day in the Life."

They were different. John was sly and scathing and quick
and at dark-side remove. Paul was more optimistic, bright-
size life, organized, romantic, and not so funny. The song
conveys some of those differences in the middle verse with
Paul's contrasting fragment of autobiography, a songwriter's
parlor piece he'd held in reserve for some time. (Three of his
eight lines begin with the words "Found my.") Paul describes
himself as an adolescent schoolboy waking up from a deep
sleep and—while still half muzzy—clothing, grooming, and
feeding himself, then hurriedly catching the bus to begin
the morning. I like that Paul, with his transcendent gift for
melody, here talk-sings. The language is so bouncy and
active it creates a physical intimacy that bends toward the
existential meditations of John. (When Paul runs for the
bus, John supplies the heavy breathing.) The beat is now
peppy with drum and snatches of piano, a common Beatles

rhythm. And in describing a person getting from bed to bus, this could just as well be somebody leaving for work or anywhere else. Nothing could be more banal, just another day in the life caught in eight perfect lines.

And then he's smoking (something) and we are back into a (cosmic) dream, back to John with his newspaper. And what does he find? A government tally of imperfections in the surface of English roads. His mention of Blackburn, Lancashire, gives the song the advantage of a memorably specific place name that is in service of a more general emotion—one of those strange alchemies that just happens to work in music. Think: Paul Simon's Saginaw in "America" or Jackson Browne's Winslow, Arizona, in "Take It Easy" or Neil Young's Redwood in "Heart of Gold," or Jimmy Webb's entire conception of Wichita in "Wichita Lineman." That the government really was out there in Blackburn, Lancashire, counting potholes was the sort of activity that appealed to Lennon's absurdist northern sense of humor. What did it all add up to? Four thousand! What did it all really add up to? A nonsense line about the relationship between holes and Royal Albert Hall seating capacities. Except decay, holes, people as holes, emptiness, and audience—it's another mystery almost seen. The feeling is rather sad.

These vocal sections were written and recorded first, with the empty linking section between the first John and Paul verses counted off bar by bar and then marked off with an alarm clock to get to later. The clock was there because John had brought it into the studio to tease Ringo with. Some-

thing about keeping him awake. To fill the empty space, they
drew on their producer George Martin's vast musical knowledge. (George Harrison had a similarly expansive musical intelligence, but at the time he was the one who needed a
wake-up call. The Quiet One was often inexplicably absent
while they were creating this song, and his chief contributions are the early guitar line discreetly scaffolding John and
Ringo and, it has been speculated, the choral quality of the
"Ahhh"; George Harrison loved a chorus.) So here, as at so
many times, it was everybody's good luck that Martin had
the sort of resourceful mind that could take something a
writer described in the abstract and help him express it with
sounds. John wanted "a musical orgasm." Soon enough, half
an orchestra of leading London classical musicians was assembled at Abbey Road Studios with instructions to play
their instruments from lowest note to highest, navigating
the allotted bars at their own pace. George Gershwin's *Rhapsody in Blue* begins with something similar, a solo clarinet
glissando that was itself improvised at a rehearsal by the musician. In "A Day in the Life," the idea was that the orchestra
would slide up the scale microtonally, a free-form crescendo
of accumulating pitches.

That recording session became a sixties happening, with
Beatles' friends like members of the Rolling Stones and the
Monkees and their sexy wives and girlfriends (like Pattie
Boyd and Marianne Faithfull) turning out in the trippy rega-
lia of the time. The orchestra wore proper dress-performance
clothes. In an effort to lower the class barriers between

classical and rock musicians (and also because they could), the Beatles handed out novelty-shop gag items: clown noses (for the very upstanding violins), plastic spectacles (for the more ebullient woodwinds and brass), wigs, balloons, whistles. Paul conducted in butcher apron and groovy tie. It was a high-meets-low affair in which the Beatles took careful note of the relationship between the personalities of the classical musicians and their instruments: the violins were indeed prim and possibly high-strung; the horn players struck Paul as more fun—brassy. It was a big production to buttress the song's big themes, and the inventive sound produced by the classicists for the rockers improved the reputations of both. They were all making music for the Everyman. Because the next vocal section was Paul's—about a guy waking up—in the end, they kept the alarm clock.

After John's reprise, the orchestra returns for an even greater swelling of sound. It was like something blowing up, a tremendous wreck, the explosion of a gun inside a car. And then, after all the chaos and destruction, what next? George Harrison had suggested a fade to humming. But it didn't work. Paul thought that the song needed firmer resolution. Four Steinway pianos and a harmonium were rolled into action, and at every keyboard the players were instructed to hit the single chord of E major simultaneously and hard, with the loud foot pedal down, letting it carry as long as possible. There were nine takes. The tone is big, so capacious and resonant because Martin and Emerick thought to put the recorder on half speed. It's the sound of peace. Instead of love being all you need, here it's music that gets you through all the days and nights.

By now, the Beatles' new songs were often so complex they didn't translate as well to public performance, and they'd become a studio group. Other musicians took notice. Like all much-admired, well-known works of art, "A Day in the Life" means many things to many people. To writers, it's a clinic of craft, every detail fussed over, worked and reworked with migraine intensity and forbearance, unlikely connections fused into logic, all the beautiful segues. Before Brian Wilson, before Lennon and McCartney, that's not how rock musicians were supposed to do it. Nonchalance was part of the act. But after "A Day in the Life," it soon became acceptable for rock musicians to strain at their songs with the same laborious compulsion that Giacometti brought to a portrait. The Who was writing rock operas; Jimi Hendrix labored over *Electric Ladyland*.

But it wasn't just the permission to be a perfectionist. It was the understanding that musicians could be as ambitious for the content of rock songs as other artists were in mediums like literature and painting. In all cases, what you are trying to do is move past literal life into the imagination to render the *almost*—to express the mysterious ambiguity that is more deeply life. As Giacometti told his biographer James Lord, "The more you struggle to make it lifelike the less like life it becomes. But since a work of art is an illusion anyway, if you heighten the illusory qualities, then you come closer to the effect of life." The illusion of something ordinary becomes something eternal, the forever day—and the song of a lifetime.

I AM THE WALRUS

BEN ZIMMER

"It seems very pretty," she said when she had finished it, "but it's rather hard to understand!" (You see she didn't like to confess, even to herself, that she couldn't make it out at all.) "Somehow it seems to fill my head with ideas—only I don't exactly know what they are!"

—ALICE, upon first reading
"Jabberwocky," in *Through the Looking-Glass*

INSPIRED NONSENSE HAS HELD ME in its spell for as long as I can remember. Growing up in a house full of books, I spent the most time with the ones that were seriously silly. I graduated from Dr. Seuss to *The Complete Nonsense of Edward Lear,* a well-thumbed Dover paperback adorned with Lear's own absurd pen-and-ink drawings, so you could see just what he meant by *the dolomphious duck* and her *runcible spoon*. And I dove deep into *The Annotated Alice*, Martin Gardner's illuminating exposition of Lewis Carroll's Alice books, its margins bursting with side notes that made the curious main text even curiouser.

My parents, enlightened children of the sixties, also had John Lennon's *In His Own Write* on the shelf, and though it didn't make much of an impression on me at the time, I recognized a kindred spirit. John, too, must have grown up cherishing the surreal, imagistic language of Lear and Carroll. But his greatest work of nonsense was not on our bookshelves, of course. It was over in the record cabinet, on the raucously colorful *Magical Mystery Tour* LP: "I Am the Walrus," the final track of side one.

A sonic childhood memory: the turntable on our Heathkit stereo spins, and I hear John's electric piano wobbling between two notes. The strings enter forebodingly. Ringo's drums kick in. And then John, continuing the two-note wobble with his thin voice, delivers that recital of deceptively simple words, with *I, you, he, me*, and *we* all coming together. I got that right away, or thought I did. At least it was easier to grab on to, at age seven or eight, than mouthfuls like *crabalocker fishwife* or *semolina pilchard*.

The LP had lyrics for some of the songs in the gatefold, and I began studying them as the record played. Like Alice reading "Jabberwocky," my head filled with half-formed ideas. I remember wishing that Martin Gardner had done for "I Am the Walrus" what he had for Carroll's nonsense. In

Through the Looking-Glass, Humpty Dumpty, that master of words, offers some dismissive explanations of "Jabberwocky" to Alice. But Gardner's annotated version breaks out of the narrative walls with a flurry of commentary—twenty-four numbered notes for "Jabberwocky" alone. So if you follow the note for *uffish* you can read what Carroll himself said about the word in a letter to a young friend: "It seemed to suggest a state of mind when the voice is gruffish, the manner roughish, and the temper huffish."

There were no annotations for the lyrics, but it soon dawned on me that John had playfully built in his own kind of side notes, embedding links between the song and other works. The bit about flying like Lucy in the sky linked back to "Lucy in the Sky with Diamonds," obviously enough. (Quick, pull out the *Sgt. Pepper* LP!) Later, delving into the White Album, I found "Glass Onion" linking back to "I Am the Walrus"—among other Beatles songs—with that lovely bit of misdirection *The walrus was Paul.*

Of course the walrus was John, and wait a minute, wasn't there a walrus in *Through the Looking-Glass*? Like the Jabberwock and the frumious Bandersnatch, the Walrus only appears in a text within Carroll's text: a poem recited by Tweedledum and Tweedledee. "The Walrus and the Carpenter" isn't as nonsense-heavy as "Jabberwocky," but one verse is beautifully meaningless:

> *"The time has come," the Walrus said,*
> *"To talk of many things:*

Of shoes—and ships—and sealing wax—
Of cabbages—and kings—
And why the sea is boiling hot—
And whether pigs have wings."

A walrus expounding on the flying potential of pigs? That must have made as much of an impression on the young John Lennon as it did on me. In the lyrics, pigs are flying, or things are flying like pigs, just like Lucy in the sky. Or are they running? *See how they run* makes yet another link back to childhood, to the three blind mice running from the farmer's wife. (Paul got in on the act in "Lady Madonna," quoting *See how they run* to make a joke about how both children and stockings run.)

As a budding exegete of "I Am the Walrus," I never got much further than spotting allusions to Lewis Carroll, nursery rhymes, and other Beatles songs. In the later verses, I could feel the song pushing back at me, or anyone who might dare pick it apart. The "expert-texpert" is advised that "the joker" just might be laughing at him. And then the voices in the background chortle in ridicule.

Well, what can I say? I ignored the laughter and grew up to be an expert-texpert anyway.

Magical Mystery Tour is one of my favorite albums, because it was so weird. "I Am the Walrus" is also one of my favorite tracks—because I did it, of course, but also because

it's one of those that has enough little bitties going to keep
you interested even a hundred years later.

—JOHN LENNON to Dennis Elsas,
WNEW-FM, September 28, 1974

AS I GOT OLDER and devoured book after book about the
Beatles, some stories about "I Am the Walrus" spoke to me
more than others. I didn't much care to hear about how "the
Eggman" supposedly came from a nickname for Eric Burdon of the Animals, thanks to his penchant for breaking
eggs on his sexual conquests (or, as Burdon later clarified,
having eggs broken on *him*). I preferred to think of Humpty
Dumpty as the original Eggman.

I did enjoy the recollection of Pete Shotton, Lennon's
school chum and fellow Quarryman, who explained the ori-
gins of the "yellow matter custard" that disgustingly drips
from a dead dog's eye. It was based on a British playground
rhyme that went *Yellow matter custard, green slop pie, all mixed*
together with a dead dog's eye. On my American playground, we
had a gross-out song like that, too, but it started off with
Great green globs of greasy, grimy gopher guts.

Shotton further explained that the memory of "yellow
matter custard" was sparked by a letter to Lennon from a
student at Quarry Bank, their old high school in Liverpool.
The student said that his literature class was analyzing

lyrics to Beatles songs, which Lennon found utterly ridiculous. The image of a "Quarry Bank literature master pontificating about the symbolism of Lennon-McCartney" inspired him to come up with "yellow matter custard" and similarly cockeyed lines. As Shotton tells it, after Lennon wrote down the line about "semolina pilchard" unaccountably scaling the Eiffel Tower, he smiled and said, "Let the fuckers work that one out, Pete!"

Fine, then. Maybe the song is just a put-on, or a kind of a dare. No wonder I felt like it was resisting me. It is endlessly analyzable, and yet somehow analysis-proof. Any interpretive effort runs aground on the limits of interpretation. Lennon sneers at the overanalyzing expert-texperts like that Quarry Bank literature teacher who would kick Edgar Allan Poe if given half a chance.

To further tantalize literary types, at the end of the song we hear a scene from *King Lear* in the background, with Oswald's final words, "O, untimely death!" standing out. (That line ended up as grist for the "Paul is dead" conspiracy mill, of course.) As it turns out, the performance of *Lear* just happened to be on a radio that was tuned to the BBC while they were mixing the song. The studio engineer, Geoff Emerick, said it was Lennon's idea to get some "random radio noise" from "twiddling the dial," an injection of John Cage–style found audio. Talking about the song with New York radio DJ Dennis Elsas, Lennon claimed he "never knew it was *King Lear* until years later" when someone told him.

People read too much into Lewis Carroll, too, as Martin

Gardner, my guide through the looking-glass, pointed out in an annotation to "The Walrus and the Carpenter." Carroll gave the manuscript of the poem to the illustrator John Tenniel, telling him that he was free to make the walrus's companion a *carpenter*, a *butterfly*, or a *baronet*, since any of those dactylic words would fit the meter. Tenniel picked the *carpenter*. Let that serve as an antidote, Gardner advised, to "the tendency to find too much intended symbolism in the *Alice* books."

But isn't it the human condition to find meaning in even the most arbitrarily assembled words and sounds? At least it's *my* condition.

What about the song's first line, *I am he as you are he as you are me and we are all together*? If you want to find a precursor in Carroll, you could, as Walter Everett does in *The Beatles as Musicians*. When Alice goes down the rabbit hole in *Alice's Adventures in Wonderland*, she suffers an identity crisis, wondering if she might have turned into her sister, Mabel: "Besides, *she's* she, and I'm I, and—oh dear, how puzzling it all is!"

Others point to "Marching to Pretoria," a song dating back to British soldiers in the Boer War. Some versions of the old tune go "I'm with you, and you're with me, and so we are all together." Could Lennon have heard one of these versions and riffed on it, consciously or subconsciously? He never said, though he did tell *Playboy* that he wrote the first line of "I Am the Walrus" on an acid trip one weekend in 1967, and the second on an acid trip the next weekend.

George Harrison, for his part, told Beatles biographer Hunter Davies in 1968 that the first line of "I Am the

Walrus" was a good example of people taking the Beatles too seriously. "It's true, but it's still a joke. People looked for all sorts of hidden meanings. It's serious and it's not serious." That reminded me of Paul McCartney's own preemptive strike against meaning-mongers in the introduction to Lennon's *In His Own Write*. "There are bound to be thickheads who will wonder why some of it doesn't make sense, and others who will search for hidden meanings," McCartney wrote. "None of it has to make sense and if it seems funny then that's enough."

But if we allow ourselves to get serious and scholarly, there's another way to think about that first line: as a play of pronouns and shifting perspective that expressed the culmination of lyrical trends the Beatles had been exploring since their early days. This hadn't occurred to me until I read *The Secret Life of Pronouns* by the social psychologist James Pennebaker. As part of his demonstration of how pronouns and other function words serve as "keys to the soul," Pennebaker plumbs Beatles lyrics and finds that over time they grew "more complex, more psychologically distant and far less positive." Their pronoun use shifted, with first-person singular pronouns— *I* and *me*—dropping from a rate of fourteen percent in the Beatles' first years to seven percent in their final three years. ("I Me Mine," Harrison's first-person foray at the very end of the band's existence, was a bit of an outlier.)

When Lennon and McCartney started writing original songs, *I* was invariably paired with *you*. As McCartney explained in the *Anthology* documentary series, "All our early songs had always had this very personal thing," such as "Please Please Me," "P.S. I Love You," "From Me to You," and "Thank You Girl." But a shift began to occur in the summer of 1963, he said, when they collaborated on "She Loves You." "We hit on the idea of doing a kind of a reported conversation: 'I saw her yesterday, she told me what to say, she said she loves you.' It just gave us another little dimension, really."

What can combining first-, second-, and third-person pronouns in one song accomplish? If done well, it can create a kind of personal identification, an empathy, shared across the boundaries of the singer, the imagined listener, and the world of the song. Lennon's "Nowhere Man," from 1965, is a bit too on-the-nose in this department: *Isn't he a bit like you and me?* The show of identification feels forced. But two years and who knows how many acid trips later, Lennon could find new profundity (pseudo or no) in the string of pronoun equations that opens "I Am the Walrus." First-person *I* equals third-person *he*, second-person *you* equals third-person *he*, second-person *you* equals first-person *me*. Then fuse all of the above into an inclusive first-person plural *we*. All together now. That's some serious unseriousness.

But even nonsense words have to come from somewhere, there must have been a thought process that threw them up.

—HUNTER DAVIES on "I Am the Walrus,"

in *The Beatles Lyrics* (2014)

———

NONSENSE COMES in many shapes and sizes. You can use relatively plain language to conjure absurd or incongruous images, like the act of sitting on a cornflake. You can juxtapose words that don't seem like they belong together, like *semolina* and *pilchard* (coarse wheat and sardines, an odd mix—though Hunter Davies says they were both "foods from the fifties that we all hated"). You can make new, silly-sounding words by playing with preexisting ones, like rhyming *expert* with *texpert*, or melding *crab* and *locker* into *crabalocker*. Or you can make goo-goo noises.

Lennon fills out the chorus with the purest of nonsense. In the lyrics printed in the *Magical Mystery Tour* gatefold, it says GOO GOO GOO JOOB, but most prefer to transcribe it as *goo goo ga joob* or *goo goo g'joob*. The third syllable is unstressed, both in terms of the syncopated meter and the phonology of the nonsense words, so it's not a full-fledged *goo*.

It's unforgettable gibberish, though it often gets mixed up in people's memories with *coo coo ca-choo* from Simon and Garfunkel's "Mrs. Robinson," as the two songs came out around the same time. "I Am the Walrus" was recorded in September 1967 and released on record that November. *The Graduate* hit movie theaters in December, featuring an early partial rendition of "Mrs. Robinson," but the complete version with *coo coo ca-choo* in it didn't come out until April of the following year, on the album *Bookends*. So Paul Simon might have been nodding at Lennon, but not vice versa.

Some Beatle-ologists claim that *goo goo ga joob* is taken from James Joyce's stream-of-consciousness epic, *Finnegans Wake*. It certainly sounds Joycean, and it would be nice to think of "I Am the Walrus," *Finnegans Wake*, and Carroll's Alice stories forming a kind of wordplay-laden intertextual triangle. *Finnegans Wake*, after all, has many echoes of Carroll, and the eggman Humpty Dumpty figures in it as well, with his great fall paralleling the Fall of Man. One would-be expert-texpert on the Turn Me On, Dead Man website wrote that *goo goo ga joob* are "the last words uttered by Humpty Dumpty before his fall."

The closest you'll find to those words in *Finnegans Wake*, however, are *googoo goosth* in a passage that has nothing to do with Humpty's fall. That bit of goo-goo talk has more to do with the words *goose* and *ghost*, as the passage alludes to an Irish fairy tale about King O'Toole, whose old goose is miraculously made young again by St. Kevin. In the book, Joyce's protagonist, Earwicker, disturbs the sleep of Kate the cleaning woman, and when she awakes she wonders if she has seen "old Kong Gander O'Toole of the Mountains or his googoo goosth" (his goose/ghost). Could Lennon have randomly plucked *googoo goosth* from the middle of *Finnegans Wake* and changed it to *goo goo ga joob*? It's pretty implausible, especially since I know of no evidence that he ever read the book, or even riffled through its pages.

Poking around online, I discovered even more far-fetched theories about *goo goo ga joob*. A Canadian proponent of the "Paul is dead" school of thought takes the cake: "In Inuit it means 'Living is easy with eyes closed' and was used to establish a connection to the Inuit. The reason for that is that the Inuit see the walrus as a symbol of death." There is not a shred of truth to this, and it is fair to say Lennon was not studying Inuit animal symbolism, anyway. (The notion that the walrus symbolizes death can be traced to a 1969 article in the University of Michigan student paper satirizing the then new search for "Paul is dead" clues. It claimed that *walrus* was Greek for "corpse," among other bogus factoids.)

Joyce and the Inuit notwithstanding, I eventually zeroed in on a more likely source of inspiration for *goo goo ga joob* (and Simon's *coo coo ca-choo*) in popular music. The phrase shares the syncopated cadence and childlike frivolity of *boop-oop-a-doop*, made famous in the 1930s as the catchphrase of everyone's favorite cartoon pin-up, Betty Boop. Less well-remembered is Helen Kane, billed as the original "Boop-Boop-A-Doop Girl," who inserted the phrase into such hit songs as "I Wanna Be Loved by You" from 1928. (Marilyn Monroe's cover in *Some Like It Hot* preserved that song for posterity.)

Musing about the roots of *goo goo ga joob* and *coo coo ca-choo* in *boop-oop-a-doop* led me down an Alice-like rabbit hole of musical history. Who was really responsible for the nonsense phrase? In 1934, Helen Kane actually sued the makers of the Betty Boop cartoons for $250,000 in damages, claiming that they had stolen the phrase from her act. But as *The New York Times* reported, her case fell apart when a theatrical manager testified that "Baby Esther, a Negro girl under his management, had interpolated words like 'boo-boo-boo' and 'doo-doo-doo' in songs at a cabaret here in 1928, and that Miss Kane and her manager had heard her there."

When the judge was presented with a sound film of Baby Esther, that was enough for him to decide against Miss Kane. Unfortunately, that film was not preserved, and there are no other sound recordings of her. I would have loved to hear if Baby Esther's *boo-boo-boo/doo-doo-doo* interpolations had the same syncopated pattern as *goo goo ga joob* with that extra little unstressed syllable.

Baby Esther herself is a mysterious figure. One press account of the 1934 trial gave her full name as Esther Jones. But it's possible that this was a pseudonym for one Gertrude Saunders, who was referred to as "the original Boop-Boop-A-Doop Girl" in African American newspapers later in the 1930s. Yet at the time of the trial, Baby Esther was presumed to be dead. Online, the story has been obscured even further by false identifications of Baby Esther in photos and sound clips. The ultimate origin of *boop-oop-a-doop*, and by extension *goo goo ga joob*, remains elusively out of reach.

Once again, interpretation has its limits. Still, searching for the roots of syncopated baby talk, even if ultimately fruitless, reveals a fascinating chain of appropriations and reappropriations across races and cultures. Nonsense can contain its own historical sense, though the history may always be incomplete.

I can't help seeking that sense in nonsense. The urge might be genetic, as I see it replayed now in my son Blake, who started up his own Beatles obsession around the age of five. He's ten now, and is skilled in a kind of information gathering that I could only have dreamed of at his age. My wished-for lyrical annotations and textual linkages are now commonplace online, thanks to sites like Wikipedia and Genius. I asked Blake where he would look if he wanted to understand the lyrics to "I Am the Walrus," and his answer said it all: "Goo goo ga Google." But even with the never-ending electronic stream of information and interpretation that can be served up instantaneously through a search engine, the song stubbornly stands on its own, perplexing new generations of listeners with its delightful opacity.

DEAR PRUDENCE

DAVID DUCHOVNY

I'M GONNA DO THIS from memory. I'm not gonna listen to the song again, because this is about memory, the song in my head. Maybe I'll get the words wrong or the sequence, but that's the music of my mind. There's the Beatles song on the record and the Beatles song in my mind. This is the latter.

The guitar. You'd have to call it Beatlesque. But that's not what I thought when I was nine or ten. It was ringing and beautiful. And haunting. It's pretty, but sad. It's not hard to play, but I didn't know that. Most of the songs I would've liked at ten were catchy and upbeat. "Sugar, Sugar" by the Archies comes to mind. "Grazing in the Grass." "Crocodile Rock." A ten-year-old boy's ears have no pretension or shame. But something about this guitar riff is calling me, pulling at my heart. This isn't a single. It's a song. There's a moment when you start to grow up and you stop listening for singles and start listening for songs. This may have been mine.

And then the words—*Dear Prudence, won't you come out to play?* Prudence. Not a common name. Not easily rhymed, like Barbara Ann, or Renee who walked away. A name that is of a quality like Patience or Chastity or Honor. A girl's name. A name that means caution or wherewithal or looking before you leap. This is a girl who has trouble letting go. I relate to that. The ten-year-old boy relates to that field of back-and-forth with his parents and teachers. And the singer, it's John, he's nasal but full of care, he addresses Prudence as dear, he likes her, he cares for her, he respects her, he wants her to come out to play. There's the turn already. He wants Prudence, full of worry, to let go a little and play. It's all there in the first line. Something is inhibiting Prudence and John is asking her, he's not demanding, he's not the John of "I Want to Hold Your Hand." He's very courtly—*Dear, Miss* . . . is he writing a letter? He's being gentle with Prudence. He's being prudent.

Why? So she can meet the brand-new day. Well, you can't fight that logic. Maybe yesterday was tough for Prudence. It seems so, because she is inside and isolating herself. And John is saying: It's okay; it's a new day. And *look outside*. He talks about the sun and sky. Go on, Prudence, just look out the window. And then he tells her that the day is beautiful and so is she. It's all terribly simple. And now Prudence is beautiful, but it doesn't feel sexual. She is beautiful like the sun and the sky. She's alive like the world and should take part. And then John brings it full circle, asking again if she won't come out to play. He's gentle, yes, but he's not giving up.

And Prudence is not easily convinced. She needs another

verse. Then the second verse begins, but now Paul's bass starts heaving, bringing an entirely new energy into the equation. The bass sounds like a pumping heart or deep breaths, insistent where John's pleading has been gentle. You feel Paul's bass in your chest. Now John asks, still courtly, if he can see her smile. That's nice. Like a little child. And the way he turns *child* into *child* with three syllables kills me to this day. He's starting to syncopate with Paul's bass, and he wants her to look outside again at the natural world, at nature. The clouds are a *daisy chain*. He wants to see her *smile again*. It's a nursery rhyme. Prudence is a young girl, or a young girl who lives on in an adult lover, but even at ten, I know I'm in a fairy-tale space and things are not as they seem. Prudence has stopped smiling for some reason. Again. She *has* smiled, but not now. What loss has she suffered? I sense an adult is to blame.

And now we enter the bridge, though it feels like falling off a cliff, and John is telling Prudence to look around, in a deeper, almost mechanical tone, drained of feeling. And as courtly as he has been, now it's dreamy and chanting. It's a whole new musical feel, like a different song, but the message is the same. Again, look outside, Prudence, you're too focused inward, that's the cause of your sadness, look at the blue sky, look at the clouds, look around. The world is beautiful because you are a part of it, not apart from it. And that last *around* feels like voices circling down literally around and around until we are back to the beginning. But now the drums and bass are interlocked and in step, driving John, whose diction is still courtly and fatherly but more rhythmical and insistent, to repeat the verse, same as the first. And when he hits on "beautiful" this time, it *is* beautiful, it's a cry now, his sympathy for Prudence has overwhelmed him, and he is reaching out. He elongates and rises up on "you" just so Prudence knows how much her pain is paining him. That liberation from self-seeking and self-doubt and from Prudence itself is just outside your door. And then we are back at the beginning, almost absentmindedly, the guitar, slipping in and out of the riff, fading into longer notes, a different song almost. Like the guitarist is looking up from his instrument because something else has his attention now; maybe it's Prudence coming out her door to play. That must be it. Maybe it's a ten-year-old boy opening up a door of his own to somewhere else.

HELTER SKELTER

CHUCK KLOSTERMAN

I'VE NEVER MET ANYONE whose favorite Beatles song is "Helter Skelter." If I did, my assumption would be that the person probably doesn't like the Beatles all that much. It's significantly less charming than the vast majority of their catalog and (maybe) the sixth-best song on their fifth-best album. John Lennon either mildly disliked it or merely thought it dumb ("That's Paul *completely*," he said dismissively during the last year of his life), and McCartney couldn't have loved it that much, either (since he never wrote another track structurally analogous in the subsequent five decades). It's a lurid outlier. Still, "Helter Skelter" cannot be marginalized as an experiment or a castoff or four and a half minutes of filler. It's the well-considered, capably executed, fully conscious manifestation of a bad idea. McCartney has tirelessly explained that he came up with "Helter Skelter" as an attempt to beat the Who at a game the Who didn't even know they were playing—Pete Townshend had told a reporter that the next Who single would be the loudest, dirtiest thing the group had ever recorded, so Paul tried to imagine what that would signify and how that would sound. Bizarrely, the single Townshend was referring to was "I Can See for Miles," which turned out to be a conventionally boring Who song. But the response McCartney projected was "Helter Skelter," which is why the Beatles have a song that intermittently resembles the blades of a lawn mower falling out of alignment after hitting a brick.

It is not their best work.

I love it. But it's not their best work, and nobody will ever argue that it is.

And yet—from a cultural, historical, nonexperiential viewpoint—the only Beatles song that matters more is "I Want to Hold Your Hand." What we get with "Helter Skelter" is the rare example of a rock song with no antecedent: it's impossible to find any tune prior that sounds (or behaves) remotely similar. It's wholly a product of McCartney's sonic imagination. Now, that doesn't automatically make it *good*. It's always possible to fail in a completely original way (there's no antecedent for "Revolution 9," either). But the central flaw with "Helter Skelter"—in essence, its lack of musicality—is eradicated by the strangeness of its potential. Since no song like this had ever existed before, "Helter Skelter" was able to generate previously nonexistent trajectories. Its influence ricocheted in arbitrary directions, and it's universally viewed (for at least one brutal reason) as the most misinterpreted Beatles song ever recorded. And Harold Bloom was right: in art, misinterpretations are always more interesting than whatever was intended.

This is why "Helter Skelter" is the most interesting Beatles song that ever was.

LIKE SO MANY PEOPLE born (a) after the Beatles broke up, but (b) before John Lennon was murdered, my first exposure to "Helter Skelter" was through a cover version. It is, apparently, a pretty easy song to learn; I can't play guitar, but I can almost play the intro to "Helter Skelter." There are yowly, off-tempo goth versions (Siouxsie and the Banshees in '78), conformist replications (Aerosmith in '75, Pat Benatar in '81), lubricated punk trash (Hüsker Dü in '86), Swedish death metal (Dimension Zero in '02), roots rock (Don Harrison in '77, Gov't Mule in 2000), an interesting take from the Canadian Bonnie Tyler (Dianne Heatherington in '80), and multiple attempts by Oasis, usually with Noel Gallagher on vocals (which is, of course, preferable to the alternative). My introduction was a version by Mötley Crüe, the last song on the A-side of *Shout at the Devil*. Nikki Sixx's motives for recording this song now seem obvious, but it was weird at the time, and my fifth-grade mind couldn't isolate the weirdest part: Was it that the Beatles had written a metal song, or was is that Mötley Crüe liked a hippie song? Both thoughts felt impossible. My knowledge of pop history hovered near zero; it would still be several years before I realized the Beatles shared vocal responsibilities (I had thoughtlessly assumed Paul sang every tune, based on one TV clip of "Yesterday"). The prospect of the Beatles *inventing* heavy metal would have seemed so absurd that I wouldn't have even wasted time disagreeing with the supposition, in the same way that I wouldn't have wasted time disagreeing with the supposition that David Lee Roth invented homosexuality. These concepts did not seem connected.

Decades later, the claim that "Helter Skelter" inadvertently spawned heavy metal has become so common that even McCartney takes credit for it. This, I think, is wrong. But only technically.

"Helter Skelter" was released in November of 1968. Black Sabbath—the first band to fully embody what metal would become—didn't even start calling themselves Black Sabbath until the following summer. So "Helter Skelter" definitely came first, and the members of Sabbath were all avowed Beatles freaks. There's no question they were familiar with "Helter Skelter" when they recorded their 1970 debut, and there's a handful of Ozzy-era Sabbath songs where a Beatles influence is palpable. But those influences can't really be traced to "Helter Skelter" (maybe the lead riff on "Paranoid," but even that's a stretch). This is the central problem with classifying "Helter Skelter" as the origin of heavy metal: it's not a heavy song. It's aggressive and metallic, but there's no gravitational pull. It's not even as heavy as "Ticket to Ride." The earliest mainstream rock track exhibiting the template for modern metal is the Kinks' "You Really Got Me" from

1964, mostly for its tempo and musical language (but also because guitarist Dave Davies sliced the back of his amp with a razor blade and distorted the entire concoction). "Purple Haze" came out in 1967. Embryonic efforts from Blue Cheer, Vanilla Fudge, and Steppenwolf also predate "Helter Skelter," and Steppenwolf literally used the phrase "heavy metal thunder" to describe whatever it was they thought they were doing. So, sure—there is a methodological flaw with asserting that the Beatles invented metal. It was not the mechanical origin. But it was the *beginning*, simply because the Beatles were the Beatles (and all those other artists were not). By virtue of who they were, the Beatles' interest in producing a tune like "Helter Skelter" validated the aesthetic premise of a raw, rabid song solely designed to make soft people recoil.

The Beatles' songbook is a neutral charge. It's a self-reflexive reality. Every other guitar band of the past sixty years has made a *kind* of rock: blues-rock or prog rock or folk rock or acid rock or punk rock or grunge rock or art rock or [*pick a modifier*] rock. But not the Beatles. The Beatles made "Beatles Music," which became the working definition of "rock music," which became the working definition of "popular music." Black Sabbath worked within a genre; Blue Cheer worked within a subgenre. The Beatles had no such parameters. They could do whatever they wanted, and whatever they did became normative. If the Beatles had prominently employed the accordion on *Revolver*, we'd all be able to walk into any local Guitar Center and stare at a wall display of accordions, most of which could be plugged into Marshall amplifiers. Anything the Beatles did immediately became something that could be plausibly attempted by other artists. The Beatles "invented" heavy metal to the same degree they "invented" the notion of a pop band breaking up in public: they weren't the first people to have the idea, but they were the first materialization of that idea in a context that collectively mattered. "Helter Skelter" *ratified* metal. Had Mötley Crüe covered "Smoke on the Water" or "Children of the Grave," the unspoken message would have been "We like metal, so we play metal music." By covering the Beatles, the unspoken message was "We like music. Metal is just the way we play it."

THE CRÜE'S 1983 VERSION of "Helter Skelter" is a rote modernization of the original song, but it directly ignores the espoused intention of its creator—it is not *dirty*. It's calculated and streamlined and extraordinarily polished, which (of course) made every traditional rock critic hate it, despite the fact (or maybe due to the fact) that it was an idealized distillation of what hair metal fans liked about hair metal. Mötley's logic was to take something old and sell it as new, marketed toward pubescent kids with no relationship to the original. But unpacking McCartney's 1968 logic is more complicated. He was trying to construct a newfangled apparatus out of broken parts; he was, somewhat perversely, trying to knit a reasonable song out of a compilation of unlikable sounds.

This is not, typically, what the Beatles did. People have used hundreds of adjectives to describe what Beatles songs sound like, but the word that categorizes them most accurately is widely considered too banal to professionally employ—Beatles songs sound *nice*. The middle eighth of "You Can't Do That" sounds nice to most people, even if they don't like rock music. The backing vocals on "I'm Happy Just to Dance with You" are nice. The piano chords on "For No One" are somber, but they're somber in a way that's still totally, irrefutably nice. I realize it seems stupid to point this out, and I realize no magazine editor would ever let a critic use the word *nice* to describe the sound of anything. It's lazy and ineffectual. Yet it's the key to the Beatles' transcendence and the fundamental quintessence of McCartney's voice: Paul McCartney makes songs that sound nice to human ears, and he sings them in a nice style. And here he is on "Helter Skelter," trying to contradict his most natural of inclinations. He wants to sound harsh and discomfiting. But he's still Paul McCartney, so he can't quite get there. The song never becomes genuinely dissonant—you can hum along with the rhythm guitar, and often with the lead. The vocal performance pushes Paul's larynx to its breaking point, but nothing actually breaks (and it always seems like John should have sung this one, anyway). A lot of what McCartney identified as "dirty and aggressive" is just haphazard and unorthodox—the song starts in the middle, the drums have no swing, and there's a trippy fade-out near the end that seems a little cliché if you're not on drugs. Most pressingly, there's a technology dilemma: The studio world of 1968 wasn't ready to capture and magnify a song like "Helter Skelter." McCartney recorded his bass parts through a hundred-watt amp, which is about four times weaker than what a modern sixteen-year-old would use for a gig in his school cafeteria. This is not to suggest that you can't capture big sounds with 100-watt amps, because you can—this was the same basic equipment Jimmy Page would use to make *Led Zeppelin II* the following year. But unlike Page, the Beatles thought more about texture than depth, so it doesn't translate. "Helter Skelter" sounds small, and even a little cheap.

But here I still am, almost five decades later, listening to "Helter Skelter" on repeat and trying to convince myself that it isn't great (and failing miserably). There is an inverted bell curve with this kind of artifact: The very first time you hear it, it sounds bizarre and fantastic. Then, over the course of many years and multiple exposures, it seems to grow incrementally stupider. Particularly during the CD apex of the late 1990s, I generally skipped over "Helter Skelter," along with many other tracks on the White Album. I effectively turned a ninety-three-minute double album into a thirty-eight-minute EP. I convinced myself it was filler. But then—as with so many other Beatles tunes from this specific period—"Helter Skelter" inexplicably started to improve.

And I use the word *inexplicably* because I can't quantify a jus-
tification as to why this occurred. Maybe I'd finally internal-
ized all the things I had read about "Helter Skelter" and
injected that data back into the music. Maybe what I liked
about music *in general* was changing, and I was suddenly
hearing something in a song from 1968 that reminded me
of 1963 (my personal obsession with the Beatles moved
backward—I initially most loved the latter albums, then the
middle period, and eventually the earliest stuff). Maybe I
was just slightly older, and thus a slightly different person.
Who knows? I would be lying if I claimed to know how this
worked. But I do know that "Helter Skelter" began to sound
unlike the way I once remembered, and I started to notice
primitive-yet-sophisticated details that might not even be
there. Repetition forces transmogrification. It took years,
but "Helter Skelter" has become a sublime anomaly that
makes me think crazy, nonlinear thoughts.

And this, I suppose, is how it happens.

"THIS IS A SONG Charles Manson stole from the Beatles,"
Bono explains on the 1988 live album *Rattle and Hum*. "We're
stealing it back." Bono's words serve as the overture for the
weakest of the Thatcher-era "Helter Skelter" covers, but the
performance is not what matters. What matters is the sentiment of the introduction—the notion that McCartney wrote
a pop song that had no inherent meaning, only to have it
interpreted as a prophetic vision of a coming apocalyptic

war that would allow a diminutive thirty-four-year-old racist to become the future king of the black race. It will never be clear how Manson came to this conclusion. He was obsessed with pretty much every song on the White Album, but his other misinterpretations made (slightly) more sense. "Piggies" could *theoretically* be about beating up cops. "Blackbird" could *theoretically* be about a racial uprising. "Revolution 9" could be about almost anything, really. But "Helter Skelter" plainly describes a British amusement park ride—it's a massive circuitous tower with a slide that wraps around the perimeter. Granted, most Americans have never seen a helter skelter, and I'm certain Manson had no clue what McCartney was straightforwardly describing. Manson was likely unfamiliar with many roustabouts from the Liverpool metro area. Still, the mental jump from "carnival attraction" to "race war" is pretty profound. Why did this happen? What made this song the accidental linchpin to multiple grisly murders, beyond the fact that the man manufacturing the misconception was a sociopath?

It would be insane to blame the Beatles for this.

But just for a moment, let's be insane.

The Beatles enjoyed confusing people. They found it hilarious, especially as they aged. When Lennon made a vocal mistake on "You've Got to Hide Your Love Away," he consciously left it on the record, amused that "the pseuds" (his slang for pseudo-intellectuals) would read something percipient into the non sequitur. That psychological playfulness is a huge part of the Beatles' charisma. But in his brilliant

1994 book *Revolution in the Head,* historian Ian MacDonald makes an astute, awkward point about the risks of confusing people on purpose: The sheer scale of the Beatles' influence raised the stakes of everything they did. "[The Beatles] came to accept accidental occurrences . . . as intrinsically valid," writes MacDonald. "Listeners were left to generate their own connections and make their own sense of what they were hearing, thereby increasing the chances of dangerous misinterpretations along Manson lines."

Now, am I *really* blaming the Beatles for the death of Sharon Tate? I am not (and neither was MacDonald, to the best of my knowledge). You can't hold an artist rationally accountable for the response of irrational consumers. Still, what we see with the legacy of "Helter Skelter" is a manifestation of something that will never fail to fascinate: the irrefutability of Beatles exceptionalism. The normal rules of logic do not apply to this group. If they were any other band, the concept of a random bozo hearing a song about a slide and concluding that it was a secret communication directing him to orchestrate mass murder would be relegated to the absolute fringe of social psychosis. The music itself would seem like a footnote to the crime, almost unrelated to the event; we would never comprehend (or even attempt to comprehend) why the cult leader randomly selected whatever song he happened to pervert. But when the band is the Beatles, we (kind of) get it, in the same way we (kind of) get it when a lone gunman is discovered to be carrying a dog-eared copy of *The Catcher in the Rye.* It does not seem retroactively outrageous that the Beatles were roped into this madness; we've grown accustomed to the impact of their cultural sway. But here's the rub—we mustn't take that for granted. It's a mind-blowing thing. It's horrific and unthinkable that it happened at all, and we must make it part of the experience. Go back and listen to "Helter Skelter" again, and don't try to isolate it from all its unadulterated consequences. Don't try to pretend all that shit never happened. Try to hear what Manson heard, even though what Manson heard *is not there*. Because this is the only song where that can be done, and that's the opposite of arbitrary.

THE BALLAD OF JOHN AND YOKO

TOURÉ

PART I. THE QUOTE

IT ALL STARTED to go wrong during an Edenic moment. It was early 1966 and John Lennon and his wife, Cynthia, and three-year-old Julian were at home in posh Weybridge, in their large mock Tudor on a hill. John was twenty-five and famous in a way no musician had been before. He was famous in a way no one on earth had been. He was way more famous than Jesus was during His lifetime, but let me not get ahead of myself. For Lennon, that rarefied level of fame was suffocating.

From the outside it looked like the best of times. A few months earlier *Rubber Soul* had come out. It was their first truly mature album—the first that featured no covers, only songs they'd written. Robert Christgau calls it "when the Beatles began to go arty." A few months in the future they would be on tour in Tokyo with dates in America to come. But they didn't know that it would be their last tour. And it all began to unspool on this day, which you could mark as the beginning of the end of the Beatles, when John was at home talking to a reporter.

Maureen Cleave of the *London Evening Standard* had long been friendly with the band. Her elegantly written story made much of how big Lennon had become. "The Beatles' fame is beyond question," she writes. "It has nothing to do with whether they are rude or polite, married or unmarried, 25 or 45; whether they appear on Top of the Pops or do not appear on Top of the Pops. They are well above any position even a Rolling Stone might jostle for. *They are famous in the way the Queen is famous.* When John Lennon's Rolls-Royce, with its black wheels and its black windows, goes past, people say: 'It's the Queen,' or 'It's The Beatles.'"*

The focus on the Beatles' fame continues throughout the piece. Lennon brings up his father, Fred, who only emerged once the group exploded. "He was here a few weeks ago," Lennon says. "It was only the second time in my life I'd seen him—I showed him the door."

The story goes on noting Lennon's cars—a Rolls, a Ferrari, and a Mini Cooper—and recounting his eccentricities. He asks Cleave what day it is. He goes on about his new-found interest in Indian music. She notes, "A huge altar crucifix of a Roman Catholic nature . . . an enormous Bible he bought in Chester, his gorilla suit. 'I thought I might need a gorilla suit,' he said; he seemed sad about it. 'I've only

*Emphasis added.

worn it twice.'" It all seems so ephemeral. But sitting there in the middle of this polite piece about the inside of Lennon's home life is The Quote. The Quote that would change the Beatles forever. The Quote that would begin their thrusting out of Eden.

At first no one really noticed The Quote. The British audience that Maureen was writing for had known John for a while and was used to his eccentricities and his sense of humor. Neither Maureen nor her editors nor her readers paid much attention to The Quote. It was not the "pull quote" that editors and designers have splayed out in big bold type to get you to read the story. Years later, Maureen said, "We were used to him sounding off like that and knew it was ironically meant."

The Quote is, of course, the "Bigger Than Jesus" quote. It's the most famous quote a Beatle ever uttered and it's misquoted all the time and it's widely misunderstood. This is what he actually said: "Christianity will go . . . It will vanish and shrink . . . We're more popular than Jesus now; I don't know which will go first—rock 'n' roll or Christianity. Jesus was all right but his disciples were thick and ordinary. It's them twisting it that ruins it for me."

THE WAY SO MANY would receive The Quote was: "The Beatles say they're bigger and more famous and more important than Jesus." It was proof of the despicable egotism of these vapid young pop stars. Now, to be sure, to many teens and twenty-somethings in the sixties, the Beatles meant a lot more than Jesus Christ. But John wasn't making a boast about the fame of the Beatles. He was doing more than musing on his own celebrity. He was talking about the impermanence of religions. He wasn't pointing out how high the Beatles had risen but rather how far the Church had fallen—remember, there's a Roman Catholic altar and a massive Bible in his home. He was noting a sociocultural change. He's saying Christianity's influence is declining because it has been corrupted by Christians—the disciples twisting Christianity ruins it for him. He's saying the social order will be overturned. And that's always a dangerous thing to prophesy. For so many people, Christianity is so deeply important to their identity that to speak of it as a thing that could vanish, which is another way of saying it could die, is shocking and frightening. For them, it's an idea that could never be uttered. And John had said it. And for that he would pay.

At the end of July 1966, a small American teen mag called *Datebook* put Paul on their cover lookin' all dreamy and put on a tagline "The Ten Adults You Dig/Hate Most" and added: "John Lennon: 'I don't know which will go first—rocknroll or Christianity!'" (Maureen hadn't put an exclamation point there. *Datebook* did. Punctuation matters. That changes it from leaning toward a thoughtful comparison of global institutions to leaning toward an overexcited brag.) That issue of *Datebook* sold more than a million copies. The Quote was all over America. And some

Americans flipped the fuck out. A DJ in Birmingham, Alabama, announced that he would no longer play the Beatles. Other DJs joined him. Then southern ministers angrily denounced them. There were Beatles bonfires. John had stepped on a land mine.

A woman I once met in Alabama told me that in rural farming communities your life is deeply influenced by the weather. It can help provide a bounty or ruin your year. It's an unpredictable force that shapes lives, and because southern rural farming people have lived under the spell of something as capricious as the weather, they developed a close relationship with God as a rock-steady bulwark in a world of uncertainty. I can understand how that could lead to people having a deep need for a strong God. The South is a place that needs Christianity and its character is deeply shaped by it. In the South, a knock on Christianity is heard as a call to war.

A week after The Quote was published in *Datebook*, the Beatles sat for a press conference where Lennon explained and apologized, but it was already too late. The Quote had taken on a life of its own. The Ku Klux Klan nailed a Beatles album to a cross and protested against them. Things got so toxic that in Memphis a firecracker went off near the stage as they performed and they thought they were being shot at. They questioned why they were touring at all. They grew to feel it wasn't worth it. Ringo later said, "John wanted to give up more than the others. He said that he'd had enough." By the end of the tour they knew it would be their last. On

August 29, at San Francisco's Candlestick Park, they walked onstage holding cameras to document the end of the touring chapter of their career. Years later Lennon wrote:

"My life with the Beatles had become a trap . . . I always remember to thank Jesus for the end of my touring days; if I hadn't said that the Beatles were 'bigger than Jesus' and upset the very Christian Ku Klux Klan, well, Lord, I might still be up there with all the other performing fleas! God bless America. Thank you, Jesus."

And with touring behind him, Lennon began to think about what doors could be opening for him. "That's when I really started considering life without the Beatles," he once said. "What would it be?"

PART II. THE END

In early 1969, almost three years to the day after The Quote, John was in Gibraltar, marrying Yoko Ono and thinking even more about a future without the Beatles. During his honeymoon he wrote "The Ballad of John and Yoko." It's fun, bluesy, uptempo—and it's a ballad in the sense that it is a story song. John referred to it as journalism perhaps because he simply tells the tale of what they'd just done—traveling around Europe, getting married, and honeymooning. But right in the middle of this bright, bouncy song is a cry for help.

Yoko has come to symbolize the Eve figure who got

everyone tossed out of Eden—the woman who ruined the Beatles for all of humanity—as if she magically seduced John away and broke up the Beatles. But the truth is that before John met Yoko he was looking for a way out. Years later he would write, "Even then (1965) my eye was already on freedom." Yoko helped him do what he had already wanted to do. "Yoko gave me the inner strength," he wrote, "to look more closely at my other marriage. My real marriage. To the Beatles. Which was more stifling than my domestic life. Although I had thought of it often enough, I lacked the guts to make the break earlier."

In "The Ballad of John and Yoko" they travel through Europe in a seemingly frantic sprint. Each verse finds them in a new country, and the pacing of the song makes it seem like a madcap journey. For most of the story, even though it's John and Yoko's honeymoon, the press is around, interviewing them in bed, critiquing their clothes, poking about. As a listener, it feels claustrophobic, probably because Lennon by then felt strangled by his fame. But then again, Lennon does know how to use the fame to his advantage when he likes—the song mentions John and Yoko's famous bed-in for peace in Amsterdam where they invited media to come into their bedroom between ten a.m. and ten p.m. in order to discuss and promote peace. It was an act of political theater that worked brilliantly.

There's a deeper game going on in the chorus. It begins with the word "Christ" and ends with "crucify me." And each time John sings those words he puts a little extra juice into them. He's calling back to the "Bigger Than Jesus" controversy. You can't truly understand this song without knowing that backstory and all that it meant to the Beatles as a catalyst for a painful public moment, which Lennon felt he should not have had to apologize for. He's jabbing his sanctimonious Bible Belt critics right in the eyes by jamming their taboo words down their throats over and over in the song. But I think he's also saying something heavier here—that he needs help: I can't continue on this path. I can't continue having the media and the world following me and judging me and being all over me. They're gonna be the death of me. I can't continue being a superfamous Beatle. I need out.

By then, the end was growing near. The relationships between the guys were strained nearly to the breaking point. By now, John perceived of Yoko as a part of the group and he insisted she sit in on recording sessions and offer opinions. This infuriated the other Beatles. But she was the man's new wife. It had to be dealt with delicately because he loved her immensely. You get a peek at why in "The Ballad." Right in the center of the song, at about the ninety-second mark, at the crescendo right after Paul does this Vegas chintzy little glissando thing on the piano, right after that, there's this great little scene. John describes a nighttime conversation with Yoko about what happens after you die and your soul goes on. In the story of the song it's the only time we really see her say or do anything, so it stands out. I can see them lying in bed, way past midnight, both nude, a cloud of weed smoke above them—they're in Amsterdam, so—and they're talking about philosophy and levels of consciousness and she's fulfilling something in his soul. He's saying: She's a deep thinker and she's opening me up and she's cool to listen to and I love her.

Paul knew what all this meant. "I must admit we'd known it was coming at some point because of his intense involvement with Yoko," he later said. "John needed to give space to his and Yoko's thing. Someone like John would want to end the Beatles period and start the Yoko period; and he wouldn't like either to interfere with the other."

Five months later, on a flight to Toronto, John Lennon decided to leave the Beatles. That day he told Eric Clapton, who was on the flight. A week later he told the rest of the group. "I'm breaking the group up," Lennon said. "It feels good. It feels like a divorce." He walked out and, according to Yoko, he said, "That's it with the Beatles. From now on, it's just you—okay?" His old Eden was dead. He was in a new Eden. He went on to make music and to make a family with Yoko. The world described by "The Ballad"—where he and Yoko are linked at the heart, dealing with love, fame, and protest art—that became his new Eden.

OCTOPUS'S GARDEN

ELISSA SCHAPPELL

WHEN I WAS A LITTLE GIRL my family use to sing Beatles songs on car trips. It sounds impossibly quaint now, but it was the seventies and my family—mother, father, sister, and me—just the four of us—sailing down the highway in our station wagon, singing—well, we were happy.

Ringo was my favorite Beatle, so I loved to sing "Yellow Submarine" and "Octopus's Garden," and it is Ringo who begins the story of the Yellow Submarine.

"In the town where I was born, lived a man . . ."

This was my father's part. Sometimes it was necessary to cajole my parents into singing; other times my father would just begin, the three of us joining in—and finally the Beatles came in for the chorus. For all I knew (and I hoped I was right), somewhere on the other side of the world people were already actually living in yellow submarines. It was trippy, but entirely possible.

It was our song.

After we finished singing "Yellow Submarine," we'd segue into "Octopus's Garden"—

"I'd like to be under the sea . . ."

—but honestly, there wasn't the same level of enthusiasm. Maybe because my dad didn't begin it? Maybe because it wasn't about the joys of living underwater with your friends and family and being happy forever, but about freedom? About being able to escape your ordinary life and run away to a place where no one could tell you what to do.

This was what made it feel like my song.

"Octopus's Garden" required the same sort of leap into fantasy, although I wouldn't have called it fantasy, but the *realm of possibility*. It was entirely possible that, if you were the right kind of person—polite, brave, and well mannered—you could make friends with an octopus. Surely if you did, the octopus—who in cartoon form is often depicted wearing a top hat and ascot, and occasionally a monocle—would invite you and your friend into his home. Octopuses are known to be house-proud. And surely if anyone could befriend a cephalopod it would be Ringo. And if Ringo were to take anyone, why not me?

"YELLOW SUBMARINE" and "Octopus's Garden" are admittedly not the best Beatles songs, but they are emblematic of a time in my childhood when the depth of my misery was being forced to pull weeds, cut grass, and rake leaves.

Later, I'd graduate to Keith Moon; there was something

exhilarating and terrifying and sexy about Moon, who re-fused to be relegated to back of the band, but rushed, as though ravenous, to meet the drums. He wasn't simply play-ing them. It was like they had come alive. Watching Moon in the throes of a jaw-dropping solo, wild-eyed and wet with sweat, his sticks a blur as he works himself into a hedonistic frenzy—he might as well be at an orgy.

But this is the opposite of what I wanted as a girl. What I wanted was to be filled up with music that made me want to dance around my parents' basement and, at the very top of my lungs, sing songs about hiding out with an octopus in a coral-protected cave. I wanted magic.

That age and those times spent listening to my par-ents' Beatles records in our basement, believing it was a place bad fortune could never find us, are among the happiest of my life.

I LIKED RINGO not only because he *wasn't* the most popular Beatle (early instance of my lifelong suspicion of whatever is most popular), but because he was the drummer (early indi-cator of my lifelong thing for drummers). Ringo was the devilish, happy prankster with the saucer-sized eyes. Beyond his role as drummer, sitting at the back of the band, yet holding everything down, Ringo always seemed slightly on the outside, a part of something, but alone, wisecracking in the background.

Still, from the way Ringo was always laughing and

clowning around, you'd never have guessed he was unhappy. Of course, later we'd hear he'd been miserable. Maybe, in that way, I recognized myself in Ringo.

IT WASN'T UNTIL I was older that I learned people could change their names. That Ringo Starr's given name was the far less glamorous Richard Starkey, or that the nickname "Ringo" came from his taste for flashy rings, and "Starr" was because his Beatle brothers called his drum solos—such as they were—"Starr-time."

THE FIRST TIME my father was diagnosed with cancer I was fifteen and it was lymphoma. A tumor the size of a small grape growing in the lymph nodes beneath his jaw. The second time I was twenty-two and it was a tumor the size of an almond in his left lung.

In order to remove the diseased part of his lung, they had to crack his rib cage.

In the sun, the large C-shaped scar on his back turned white.

After his recovery, my father—who had several times taken the family snorkeling, pointing out spiny black urchins and starfish in Jamaica, barracudas and clown fish in the Yucatán; who was always, it seemed, rescuing me or my little sister from being dashed against the reef—announced he was taking up scuba diving.

It is true that starfish can regrow lost limbs. Not only that, if the severed limb contains enough of the main body, it can regenerate. It can become a totally new starfish.

IT MAKES SENSE THAT Ringo would find a muse in the octopus. In undersea cartoon bands the octopus is always the quirky drummer. Who could resist?

One arm for the bass drum, another for the snare and hi-hat, one for a tom.

If you consider the octopus's decentralized nervous system and the fact that more than half of its neurons are located in its arms—thus its astonishing dexterity—if any creature in the kingdom could play the drums, it would be the octopus.

There is no evidence that the octopus can regrow a lost limb.

Although the octopus is almost always depicted as being goofy—it's all those silly arm-legs and the balloon shape that seems to call out for a loopy grin—to me, the octopus looks haunted and inscrutable. The octopus—despite depictions of him as a goggle-eyed roller-skating spastic, a bumbling tap dancer with eight left feet—never seemed all that comical to me, even as a girl. People thought he was ridiculous because of the way he looked and so they made him ridiculous.

Make the octopus ridiculous; go ahead—so much the better. For the octopus wants nothing more than to be left alone. In captivity octopuses are notoriously difficult and cunning. At every turn they defy their captors—be they researchers or zookeepers. Taken from their homes, they sulk, refuse to run mazes, and seemingly enjoy employing those remarkably dexterous arms to sabotage plumbing and electrical wiring.

Should they wish to elude you, they will change the color and texture of their skin. Hoping to pass for a bit of seabed when a shark slips by, they camouflage themselves by turning a pebbly mottled green. Should they be struck by desire, they will slip into something more comfortable, perhaps a skin of velvet plum and gray.

Even the octopus's most famous trait—the ability to shoot a cloud of ink (actually melanin, the pigment responsible for coloring human skin) into the face of a predator—jibes with Ringo's sense of humor.

THE STORY IS THAT Ringo was inspired to write "Octopus's Garden" while sailing in Sardinia, when the ship's captain told him of the octopus's fondness for decorating its lair with rocks, shells, bits of sea glass, and anything else that caught its fancy. Ringo was smitten.

From that time forward Ringo never again ate octopus.

As a girl, I was inspired to draw octopuses in their undersea gardens. I decorated their lairs with checkered curtains and candelabras. I also often confused the words *tentacle* and *testicle*, which provided my parents with great amusement despite the fact that no creature, even the despised mongoose, deserves to be burdened with eight testicles.

I stopped eating octopus when I watched one open a jar on YouTube.

GROWING UP SMALLER than most kids, with a sister who was smaller still, I was ever on the alert for a wave of teasing. I quickly developed a pointed wit, scarcely more harmful than a joke-shop daisy that shoots water—still, I could depend on it to at least momentarily distract my attacker, allowing me to escape.

I WASN'T GOOD AT SPORTS. Except for gymnastics. My parents, wanting to encourage me in the one sport I excelled at, set up tumbling mats and a balance beam my father had built for me, in the basement.

Our basement wasn't like a lot of my friends' basements. There was no shag carpeting or wood paneling, no pool or foosball table, and surely no TV. The concrete floors were painted bluish-gray, the back wall was exposed concrete, there was a narrow crawl space where we kept the sleds and Christmas tree stand, there was a washing machine and dryer, and overhead a network of copper pipes snaked along the low ceiling. It was cool and smelled like earth. Even so, it was a magical place to me as a girl. It was warm in the winter and cool in the summer. One could imagine, with the sound of the washing machine and footsteps overhead, that one was indeed in a cave beneath the waves.

Every night after dinner, unless there was still daylight, in which my father might go outside and walk around his yard surveying the plantings and flower beds, he would head down into the basement, and my sister and I, if our homework was done, would follow him.

My sister and I liked to play records and do gymnastics while my father welded. With mask in place and acetylene torch in hand, sparks flying around his head, our father transformed metal rods into people—a mother with two daughters—a Big Bang explosion of geometric shapes that would hang over our hearth, a life-sized man with curly hair and uncircumcised penis that brought us no small measure of embarrassment when friends came over, and fish swimming through coral. One fish, which was five feet long, commissioned by a couple whose property backed up to the woods, looked like it was swimming through the trees.

Running along the wall over my father's workbench was a pegboard hung with tools: silver wrenches whose jaws opened with the spin of a dial, screwdrivers with clear-yellow-and-black-striped handles; toothy handsaws, for trimming branches and cutting wood; and hammers—claw hammers and small hammers, and one with a rubber tip. At the very top, in the shadows up near the ceiling, was a dusty model ship my father had built in high school, a gold-and-green-painted schooner with real rigging and sails. It was a wonder. There were pieces of graph paper outlining his land-scaping plans, trying to imagine where to put this rhodo-dendron and that azalea.

No matter how many hundreds of times I poked around my father's workbench I always discovered something new. A silver can that turned cold when you shook it, a clear box containing all the rattlesnake rattles he'd collected through-out his life growing up in the Pennsylvania woods, ball bear-ing marbles, and a blue birdcage my father had carved—not five inches tall, with a yellow bird inside. The cage had no door. How could my father, even with the slimmest blade, have carved the bird inside that cage?

Every night my sister and I would *practice*. "Daddy!" we'd call out, standing on our heads. "Watch me! Watch this!" we'd shriek as we wobbled along the beam. "Want to see what I can do?" we'd yell, trying to jump up to grab ahold of one of the low-hanging pipes and do a chin-up. "Look, do you see? Are you looking?"

And my father would, very good-naturedly, always put down whatever he was doing and come over to watch us, spot my back handspring, admire our cartwheels, clap even when we slipped off the beam. *Look at how strong you are*, he'd say. *Wow, you are really getting it.* And he'd shake his head in appreciation and wonder like he couldn't even imagine do-ing a forward roll.

We played *Abbey Road* all the time. Even so, every time the song began—there was that melodic little burp of bubbles before Ringo began to sing—my sister and I would go wild, bellowing joyfully at the top of our lungs (after all, there was no one except for our father to hear us), *"We would be so happy, you and me!"*

This was the time when we believed my father could do magic.

We would still believe it, my mother, my sister, and I, when my father discovered the first tumor, and we would believe it until the day he died, fourteen years and two seven-year stays of remission later. For a time, I believed he might even come back. Was that a fantasy? Was that completely beyond the realm of possibility?

MY FATHER SPENT THE MAJORITY of his waking weekend hours out working in the yard. Long before we'd awake he'd have cranked up the rock and roll—Rolling Stones, Beatles, Grateful Dead—and be outside pruning trees, planting bushes, perhaps weeding the flower bed, although that job fell mostly to me and my sister.

I could never understand what pleasure my father got from working in the yard. It was so hot and buggy and tedious. It was unfair that I was not allowed to weed the grass in my bikini, or operate the chain saw.

I did, however, love our yard. Behind our house were woods—walnut and poplar trees—and, in front of a split-rail fence, a long bed of overflowing flowers and painted grasses, and swaying stalks of freckled yellow, pink, and purple foxgloves who opened their mouths like dragons when we pressed the sides of the flower. Magenta coneflowers sprang up straight, and silvery lamb's ears laid low. There were violets, and pink and white bleeding hearts spread out of the beds, finding their way into the woods behind our house, with the bright-orange-and-black-streaked tiger lilies, and my favorite of all—the fragrant, frilly, pink and white and red, nearly purple, peonies. My father let me cut the blooms to take to school (despite the ants sequestered between the petals), their stems wrapped in wet paper towel and tinfoil, so I could smell them all day even as I flicked ants off my desk.

In the beds beside the house grew grandiflora magnolias almost as tall as our house, with dark green leaves and enormous, fragrant cream-colored blossoms bigger than your outstretched hand, and petals soft like skin. The hill was banked with coral and pink primroses, blue-and-green-and-white-striped hostas mingling with lily of the valley and spreads of feathery ferns. In front of the house, under the walnut and dogwood trees, appeared trillium and the otherworldly-looking jack-in-the-pulpits. Behind the house, flanking the woods, were two decorative ponds full of koi, peepers, a snake or two, and occasionally, haunting the greenery, rabbits and a box turtle.

It was its own world.

THE LAST TIME I'd see my father at home, his cancer had metastasized from his lungs to his spine. The chemotherapy doubled him over with nausea. The cold of the bathroom tile made his feet cramp; it was painful for him to walk. He was, despite his best efforts, often irritable.

Even so, I asked him if he'd walk around the yard with me, and talk to me about the garden. I asked if I could film him. Yes, it felt artificial. No, I didn't know it would be the last time I'd walk around the yard with my father, or the last time he would walk through his garden.

The feeling my father said he had been going for was an English garden. "Listen," he said, "the most important thing is to do what you want to do . . ." He paused to rub his aching lower back where the cancer had begun to climb his spine. "I, personally, like the look of an English garden, but that's me. The important thing is to plant a garden *you* want to spend time in. *You*. No one else."

That spring he'd said that everything in the garden was the most beautiful it had ever been. Even the bark on the trees, he said. His peonies were glorious. Then there were the lightning bugs, which he said he thought were the greatest things in the world. And we'd stood on the deck at dusk with night coming on, watching for those pops of vivid green light burning like signal fires.

The night my father died, a white water lily bloomed in the bottom pond. Even in the moment it felt trite. That night, for the first time unafraid of the dark, I walked down to the edge of the yard and lay in the wet grass, stretching out by the flower bed. I put my hand in the dirt and let it fall through my fingers, thinking I wanted to be somewhere my father had put his hands.

THE LAST TIME I went home before my mother sold the house and moved, I walked around the yard as I had so many times before, in the daytime in the afternoon, in the dark. I rebuilt the stone wall that ran along the driveway. Shovel in hand, I roamed the property digging up plants—ferns and hostas—that would do well in the shade and a peony that wouldn't. I took a dogwood sapling and two pairs of jack-in-the-pulpits and weeds. I dug up my father's weeds, clover, and crabgrass, and transplanted them into my own garden.

Tomorrow, my father will have been dead for twenty years. I intend to work outside as I always do on this day to honor him. I will water and dig and listen to his favorite music, the music he loved best—the Rolling Stones, Neil Young, the Grateful Dead, and yes, of course, the Beatles. Especially the Beatles, so I can, if only for the time it takes to sing "Octopus's Garden," be that girl. The one who could easily imagine a world where an octopus would take you in and give you tea, where you could sing and dance around in your basement with your father forever, the one who couldn't yet understand how sometimes you cried over a song because it made you both happy and sad.

THE END ("GOLDEN SLUMBERS" / "CARRY THAT WEIGHT" / "THE END," FROM *ABBEY ROAD*)

RICK MOODY

IN 1969, my parents bought a rather grand high-fidelity stereo system for the living room in our house in the Connecticut suburbs. It was funereal, stately, ostentatious, and occupied the better part of one corner of the room. The housing, which secreted away the stereo components, consisted of some elegant finished hardwood, within which was inlaid a turntable, and a tuner, and a shelf on which to store some portion of your LP collection, and two speakers, at either end. All dolled up in the cabinet. The Joneses must have had one and we were keeping up.

Music was important in that household. My mother sang and played piano (the piano was right adjacent to the "hi-fi"), and my sister was learning guitar. I had had a brief flirtation with violin. My dad had been a classical DJ in college and had lots of opinions about Beethoven and Mahler and Brahms. He and my mother also favored the ubiquitous show tunes, *Man of La Mancha*, *South Pacific*, *Carousel*, *West Side Story*. Everyone was a listener. Everybody sang.

Mostly, the coffin-sized stereo got played right before dinner. My mother liked to put on music while laboring domestically in the kitchen, and I liked to sit around in the living room preoccupied with whatever was on. My mother's most fervently listened-to albums were by the duo Simon and Garfunkel. We had their every release, and I can remember deep engagement with *Bridge Over Troubled Water*, which still causes the hair on the back of my neck to stand up.

And then there were the Beatles.

I heard them on the radio practically from my first culturally aware moment. I can remember "A Hard Day's Night" (and that F9 chord) not long after its release, and "Eight Days a Week." "Help!" might have been the first Beatles single I contemplated as it was happening, and maybe this is indicative. I knew "Yesterday" and "Michelle," likewise. But it wasn't until the single releases in the span of *Sgt. Pepper* that I had a grip on the hysteria of the Fabs—who the artists were, what they looked like, their apostolic names. *Magical Mystery Tour*, and its related effluvia, was on heavy rotation on a small close-and-play upstairs in my bedroom, even though those songs were strange, and thereafter I was hooked. There was ample material to catch up with, and then there was the new stuff coming out. The White Album! *Let It Be!*

I don't know what prompted my mother to acquire *Abbey Road*, because she wasn't as fully committed to the Beatles as were her children. In a way, it's a measure of how demographically immense the Beatles' popularity was. The "granny tracks" that John Lennon so uncharitably (in the solo-era *Playboy* interview) disparaged among Paul McCartney's compositions lured in the likes of my mother and father. My mother was only interested in the popular song when it was very literate or musically sophisticated. Therefore, it must have been some single from *Abbey Road* that was much in evidence. Let's say it was "Something" by George Harrison, for example, which was a justifiably celebrated single from that album, with its swells of romantic feeling. (I considered myself a partisan of George above all other Beatles in those days, and I still feel awed by his unusual set of gifts—his love of augmented and diminished chords, his feel for Indian classical music, his melodic lead parts, etc.)

Whatever the cause, my mother bought *Abbey Road*, and soon it was playing on the high-fidelity stereo system with great regularity during the dinner hour. I liked to dance to it. So did my sister and brother and my mother. I can recollect, for example, dancing to "Come Together," which, while not exactly James Brown, is plenty danceable if you are eight or nine years old and just like any song that features a drum kit. I had no idea about the double entendre in the chorus.

My parents' marriage was dissolving at the time. That's the portion of the story that serves as the backdrop to this suite of songs that I'm about to describe.

I didn't know it was happening, not exactly. It is the fate of the child to adapt to the circumstances on the ground. Whether it's sheep-herding on the Mongolian steppe, or rock-throwing in Palestine, or, marital disaffiliation in the Connecticut suburbs in the early seventies, the child adapts. I knew that my parents didn't have very much to do with each other. I rarely saw them in the same room, and when I did, they didn't exactly embarrass themselves with a surfeit of affection. The arguments were few and far between, but so was the kindness. I cannot remember ever seeing my parents kiss. I assumed, as was perhaps not infrequent in the upper-middle-class enclave where we lived, that this was *just how people were.* I often had my nose in a book, or was camped out in front of the television, and I didn't consciously attend to any nearby drama that did not impress itself upon me.

The evening came when my mother sat all three of us kids down to tell us *something important,* and though there is much that I have forgotten from that time in the Connecticut suburbs, I can remember a lot about this moment—my mother's lipstick, my brother weeping and saying, "You aren't going to get divorced, are you?" before she had even finished her declaration. We were sitting in front of the fireplace in the den. It must have been a significantly uncomfortable moment for my mother, who was leaving my father, to attempt to explain her decision, and now I can feel it, that woe and misery and remorse, which I didn't feel then. My perception, while sitting there by the fireplace with her, in the den, was of resignation. My feeling was that there was nothing I could do about it. My feeling was that I was about to be an item on an itemized list of marital property. My brother wept.

Here's what I have often found in my moments of keenest disconsolation: that music has an unexpected power to console and to transmute what is most grievous. The layers of imperviousness that smother a song when you listen to it a lot, these layers are sundered away, and music is apparent in its most elemental guise, full of mystery and passion and awe. Things that you haven't heard in a fresh way in a thousand listens are suddenly bright and new, when you really need them most.

And so it was with *Abbey Road*.

One night, after the sit-down, my parents enclosed themselves in the living room at our house, in a way they had never done before, and it was in this conversation, it seems to me, that they negotiated the sundering of their union, without any of us present. There were louvered doors in the living room, which space, as I have said, also featured the hi-fi and the piano, and on this night the louvered doors were *closed*. I don't know what was said exactly, but I noticed, from upstairs, by peering down the staircase, that these metaphorically rich doors were closed, and I suspected that an end was near.

It's not that *Abbey Road* was playing that night. It's that through some metonymic action, in which a work of art becomes a symbol of all that is adjacent, *Abbey Road*, with its bright, glorious production, its elegant string arrangements, its strange and elevated moments, its harpsichord and Moog synthesizer, has become the sound, for me, of my parents separating. And in particular one passage on *Abbey Road*, when I think back now, inevitably suggests the grief about my family as no other artwork does. And it's the passage that begins with the song "Golden Slumbers."

John is alleged to have hated the "medley side" of *Abbey Road*, which was the conceptual work of Paul and George Martin. I remember my mother explaining how the songs flowed from one to the other in the medley, and my epiphanic recognition of this was first located in the fact that the theme from "You Never Give Me Your Money" turns up much later in the medley (in "Carry That Weight"). (I was also fascinated that George's "Here Comes the Sun" echoed John's "Sun King.") The *Abbey Road* medley was a gorgeous, playful, sophisticated expanse of fragments, urgent and propulsive. As others have suggested, the medley was much preoccupied with the Beatles' own dissolution, in a way that was dark and regretful—at least until the passage entitled "Golden Slumbers."

It's a lullaby! A lullaby that spontaneously appears after "Polythene Pam" and "She Came In Through the Bathroom Window." And it's because it's a lullaby that it was so powerful for an eight-year-old in a confused, resigned state. A song to soothe and mollify. And it's a particularly ancient lullaby, moreover, when you consider that the original poem on which it is based, by Thomas Dekker, was written in the early seventeenth century:

> *Golden slumbers kiss your eyes,*
> *Smiles awake you when you rise;*
> *Sleep, pretty wantons, do not cry,*
> *And I will sing a lullaby,*
> *Rock them, rock them, lullaby.*
> *Care is heavy, therefore sleep you,*
> *You are care, and care must keep you;*
> *Sleep, pretty wantons, do not cry,*
> *And I will sing a lullaby,*
> *Rock them, rock them, lullaby.*

Sometimes the oldest art has the greatest power to summon the uncanny, and maybe this was what impressed Paul McCartney, expectant father, at the sessions in question, the eternal *agape* of parental concern. Mary McCartney was to be born right after the sessions for *Abbey Road*, and no doubt his performance reflects this. Paul, as recorded, was the father who cared about the welfare of the kids in "Golden Slumbers," who lingered over the children of his domain, and it was the tenderness, the generosity, of McCartney's performance (and his summoning of the idea of *home* in the section of the lyric that he added to Dekker's original) that somehow had such an impact on me, that made me envious, that made me aware of what I wanted that I didn't even *know* I wanted, upstairs, gazing down, the idea of home.

Still, if you linger over the perfect tenderness of "Golden Slumbers," the paternal generosity of it, as with many fleeting moments in the *Abbey Road* medley, you miss what happens next, which is "Carry That Weight." With a considerably evident Ringo belting in the chorus. It would be a lie if I didn't think, as one does in troubled moments, that the idea of a *burden* being carried by a "boy" seemed, in 1970, wholly directed at me. No one else could know as I knew about carrying that weight! I took on that line from "Carry That Weight," which is the only striking bit of lyric-writing in the song, excepting the brief calling forth of an additional "You Never Give Me Your Money" verse. (Yes, one could develop an argument about "You Never Give Me Your Money" and divorce, but that would be to accord a ligamentary passage in the medley more space than it had in the original recording.) "Carry That Weight" does not endure much beyond 1:37, but it lingers as an afterimage in what follows.

The medley would not have crafted its legacy, that is to say, if it didn't land well. It would be a collection of diverse and unfinished investigations, as John Lennon worried it would be, if it didn't end dramatically. If it didn't come down with emphasis, in a commentary on what the Beatles were up to at that time. And as befits the unparalleled achievement that is *Abbey Road*, the medley comes down, therefore, on "The End."

The Beatles, in their adulthood, battle-scarred from internal struggle, had become, as adults do, exceedingly good writers of searching and reflective ballads (see "Golden

Slumbers," above, or "Let It Be," or "Across the Universe"), of the meditative, and the melancholy, of the complex. But they were, at the moment of their origin, a really great rock and roll band. Scrappy, loud, and sexy. And the moments on *Abbey Road*, like "Oh! Darling" and "Come Together" and "I Want You (She's So Heavy)," when the band trafficked in that idiom of rock and roll, are indelible moments, important moments, some of the most important moments in all of rock and roll. For me, none of these passages exceeds the compacted and cumulative power of "The End."

There's a little intro section, a mere smattering of words, and an upwardly ascending guitar figure. *Oh yeah! All right!* Played through just once, it invokes the dream register, desire and nightfall, after which "The End" (and the medley, generally) immediately does what it needed to do: it improbably yields to a Ringo Starr drum solo. As if proving that rock and roll is first of all a thing that requires *drums*. All toms! Not even a glancing cymbal in the solo, nor hi-hat, just those toms, spread wide in the stereo signal (it sounded incredibly great in the living room, when you turned the hi-fi up loud). So rare are the drum solos on rock and roll studio albums that they have an especial intensity when they do come to pass. Ringo, it is said, especially resisted solos. This one was crafted from an ensemble instrumental passage, from which everything else was stripped out. It is blunt, simple, and incredibly forceful.

But even the drum solo is not the *final word* on "The End." The song, as an ending, has to end even more dramatically than it might have done here. So: first Ringo falls back into his backbeat, his groove, and then bass and rhythm guitar enter, on the I–IV, of course. A7 to D7, if you want to be specific (there's a whole argument about how the medley is in A when it's about "greed" and in C when it's about the triumph over greed), and that's when something additionally important happens, perhaps something more than important.

What is it about the I–IV chord progression that's so lasting? Well, it's modal, yes, so you never have to leave the home key, and you can drone as much as you want, which is why Lou Reed liked it so much (on, for example, "I'm Waiting for the Man" and "Heroin"), and it's easy to learn on the guitar (especially if the song is in E: see, for example, "Gloria"), and it somehow permits all the old folk melodies. It has been used in every era of the popular song. In this case, it's as if the Beatles are going back over the entirety of their career, finding what is the lowest common denominator of everything they ever played together, at the Cavern Club, in Hamburg, at Shea, in all those studios, and up on the roof, the I–IV. If you were to try to describe, to some sequestered person, raised on the fabled desert isle, who had never heard rock and roll, what it was, and why it saves lives, you might begin by trying to describe melodically the I–IV. You might say that it's the minimum of melodic development to still qualify as development, rock and roll style. And so: this is where Paul situated his climactic moment of the medley, right here on the I–IV, and it's like those moments on Van

Morrison albums when you can hear Van shout to the band behind him, *One four!* which means *Play on.* As with Al Green's church revivals, when he just wants to feel the word of God, when he wants to let go and testify, and he looks at the band, and they know it's I–IV. This part of "The End," which some people describe as the last moment when all the four Beatles recorded together in a studio, is like that, it's like the word of God, if the word of God were a thing explicable only in guitar, bass, and drums, the most infernal racket that is the most divine racket.

And let me say something about the seventh chord. That flatted seventh is *so Beatles.* Most I–IV progressions, like when Lou Reed played them, avoid the flatted seventh, but to play the "accidental" seventh with the gusto that the Beatles played it (there are lots of these sevenths in the *Revolver* period) is to summon up the tradition of the blues, and soul music, and black music generally, and to make that gesture part of the ending on "The End" is to remember the role that black music played in who the Beatles were: commentators on the whole expanse of the popular song, and even beyond. Not capable of being confined by British popular music, or psychedelia, or Baroque music, or Indian music, or anything else, but magpies, claiming whatever shiny thing seized them, and refining and repurposing it.

Here is the I–IV as if it were written on a scroll, or on parchment, over which the Horsemen of the Apocalypse ride in, the tripartite guitar solo section. The infamous

Paul-George-John guitar showdown at the end of a long and winding career.

It is fair to say that there was not a perfectly proficient improviser in the band, remarkable though they were. Paul was probably the best instrumentalist in the Beatles, but he was most effective on the bass. George was an exceptionally beautiful lead guitar player, as I have said, but more as a composer of melodies on guitar, more as a microtonal note bender and slide player, than as a guy who could just whip off a great solo. The most technically accomplished guitar solo on any Beatles album is perhaps Clapton's solo on "While My Guitar Gently Weeps." George would never have written a part like that. He wrote out his parts for the songs to adorn the songs, not for the display of virtuosity, and he perfected them, labored over them, like a great composer. And that's why his parts are so sublime. (Compare, for example, the two extant solos on "Let It Be." Two completely lucidly thought-out solos. And utterly different.)

And John was no kind of guitar player at all. John was an unsurpassed writer, and an incredible singer. A singer of richness and singularity and emotive power. But he was not a guitar player of much note. Nevertheless, they were going to do this thing, these three men, and they were going to do it in a really inventive way: by playing two bars of a solo each, in rapid succession—Paul, then George, then John. Two bars! An abbreviated space! The solos are *astoundingly good*, and if you go online and watch all the many, many times that Paul

McCartney has reconstituted live this particular passage of music in the decades since, you will learn, inferentially, how great the recorded solos are, because no matter how road-tested Paul's band is now, and no matter how spectacular are his guest players (e.g., Dave Grohl), he cannot best the performance of the three internally feuding Beatles. Paul is all spiky and sharp on the recording, like he was in the mid-sixties, while George is given to improbable melodic leaps of huge intervals, like a slide player, and John is a rhythm guitar noise factory. They only have the two bars to develop each musical thought, and they develop them quickly, with great mastery, in the context of the *group*. They develop the ideas *together*.

To me, almost no moment in rock music is more epiphanic, more shamanic, and more transporting than this little piece of the medley. It's a demonstration of what rock and roll is, and it *derives* rock and roll, like rock and roll is a mathematical theorem. And then, after the tremendous noise assault of John's last two bars, a swooping string section and piano part come in, the whole thing swerves back into George Martin–style chamber pop, and Paul reduces down the medley and the album and the decade of the sixties and the oeuvre of the Beatles to one essential *equation* about the nature of love: *what you take = what you make*. All of the entire career of the Beatles, all those love songs, all those experiments, boiled down to the equation.

What did the equation mean to a kid in the suburbs, the

equation of that last line of "The End"? It was a comparable gesture to "All You Need Is Love," which I also thought was exceedingly deep. "The End" and its equation attempted to demonstrate that the whole troubadour history of the popular song, in which the eminences of song were strolling minstrels singing under the windows of particularly fetching noblewomen, for example, could be restated in a few simple ways. Love, as transitive verb, or perhaps as philosopher's stone, was passed from hand to hand. Love, the equation remarks, *is* a restatement of the Golden Rule, the Golden Rule as some universal constant, and it makes clear that the goal of life is to *total up* evenly, and to recognize that that evenness, the ultimate serenity of love, constitutes a kind of moral vision. Perhaps, to myself, sitting at the top of the stairs, watching the louvered doors of the living room, beyond which there was the hi-fi, the equation made clear, even in a down moment, that at some point the whole depletion of love and warmth and loyalty and common purpose was going to *balance out*. That could be relied on. No matter how harrowing the moment, things would get better.

If you think of the songs that the Beatles wrote on *Abbey Road* about how hard it was to be a Beatle at that time (George's "Here Comes the Sun," Ringo's "Octopus's Garden," Paul's "You Never Give Me Your Money"), it's nonetheless possible to see the equation of "The End" as yet another example of the yearning for something better that those four guys managed exceedingly well when they were at their very best. And that's part of why "The End" feels so sublime, when it winds up into the sinewy George Harrison solo that closes it (in the company of some winds and some horns); even in the midst of bitterness and distrust, there is, nonetheless, a bounty of hope.

YOU KNOW MY NAME (LOOK UP THE NUMBER)

DAVID HAJDU

PAUL McCARTNEY, like many other big fans of the Beatles, has always had trouble deciding which of the band's songs he loves best. "It's difficult to choose the favorite," McCartney has said. "You look at your songs and kind of look to see which of the ones you think are maybe the best constructed and stuff." With the values of song craft and associated stuff in mind, McCartney has, at various times, cited both "Here, There and Everywhere," the pretty, harmonically sophisticated love song from *Revolver*, and "Blackbird," the subtle, meticulous ballad inspired by Bach's Bourrée in E Minor, from the White Album, as his favorites among the songs the Beatles recorded.

Another time, in an interview he did with the Sun King of Beatles obsessives, Mark Lewisohn, for *The Complete Beatles Recording Sessions* book, McCartney made a statement that was news even to Lewisohn. He brought up "You Know My

Name (Look Up the Number)," the B-side to the 45-single release of "Let It Be" from 1970, and described it as "probably my favorite Beatles track!" For publication, Lewisohn put an exclamation point at the end of the sentence, redundantly.

It would be churlish to disbelieve McCartney, however strong the temptation to read posturing in his retroactive embrace of a piece the Beatles had kept unreleased for years and essentially dumped onto the market in their final days together. "You Know My Name (Look Up the Number)" is more typically brought up in lists of the Worst Beatles Songs of All Time, along with numbers like "Good Morning Good Morning," "Maggie Mae," "Dig It," and other trifles that the band generally saw as no more than album filler and dismissed themselves. As John Lennon described "Good Morning Good Morning" to journalist David Sheff in the *Playboy* interview he did with Yoko Ono in September 1980, three months before his death, "It's a throwaway, a piece of garbage." Then again, Lennon was mercilessly critical of a great many Beatles songs, regardless of who wrote them. "It's Only Love": "Terrible—one song I really hate of mine," Lennon said. "Run for Your Life": "A throwaway." "Hello, Goodbye": "Smells a mile away." "Mean Mr. Mustard": "A bit of crap." "Cry Baby Cry": "A piece of rubbish." "Dig a Pony": "Another piece of garbage." "Birthday": One more "piece of garbage." "Sun King": Yet another "piece of garbage."

"You Know My Name (Look Up the Number)" is among the remarkably small number of Beatles songs that Lennon and McCartney both seem to have relished, and I find it irresistibly, if vexingly, compelling myself. I've always thought of it as one of the strangest, most free-sounding and perplexing, goofiest, and un-Beatles-like of all Beatles songs. Geoff Emerick, the longtime Beatles engineer who worked on the multiple recording sessions for the track and helped Lennon edit the released version, described it, in his memoir, as "the least substantive song they ever put on tape." At the same time, as McCartney explained to Lewisohn, "it's so insane. It's not a great melody or anything, it's just unique."

The bulk of the recordings that came together as "You Know My Name (Look Up the Number)" took place over four days of sessions in May and early June 1967, during an acutely rich period for the Beatles and the pop music culture more broadly, a time when social and aesthetic experimentation was explosively voguish. The Beatles had abandoned live performances less than a year earlier, giving what would be their final concert, at Candlestick Park in San Francisco, until their unannounced (and, from street level, unwatchable) set on the roof of the Apple building in 1969, not long before they disbanded. Exploring and stretching the potential of the recording studio as their creative medium, they had recently finished their breakthrough in studio conceptualism, *Sgt. Pepper's Lonely Hearts Club Band*, and were in the midst of recording songs for what would become *Magical Mystery Tour*. They would never, collectively, be in a more expansive frame of mind.

Lennon was always attuned to inspiration from the commercial culture around him. He had taken the idea for the chorus to "Good Morning Good Morning" from a TV advertisement for cornflakes. A line in the same song, "It's time for tea and *Meet the Wife*," refers to a sitcom on BBC One. Nearly every word of "Being for the Benefit of Mr. Kite" came from phrases and images Lennon saw on a poster for Pablo Fanque's Circus Royal. (He changed the name of the horse, from Henry to Harry.) At Paul McCartney's London flat one day, Lennon found a telephone book on the piano and noticed an ad slogan printed on it: "You know the name, look up the number."

Working on his own, Lennon set the phrase to a set of simple chords—a pattern of D, F-sharp minor, G, and A—with the notion of writing "a Four Tops kind of song." It "never developed," Lennon would say. By the time he brought the piece-in-progress to McCartney, he presented it as a trippy amalgam of ad sloganeering and Indian-style chant, set to a Motown groove.

"John Lennon turned up at the studio and said, 'I've got a new song,'" McCartney told Lewisohn. "I said, 'What's the words?' and he replied, 'You know my name, look up the number.' I asked, 'What's the rest of it?' 'No, no other words, those are the words. And I wanna do it like a mantra!'"

In the first recording session, conducted on May 17, 1967, Lennon and McCartney worked with John's mantra-song conception, laying down take after take of the two of them bellowing, in a very rough approximation of Levi Stubbs and his harmony partners in the Tops, "You, you know, you know my name . . . you, you know, you know my name . . . look up the number" over thumping, utterly Lennonesque piano. Someone—perhaps, but not necessarily, Ringo Starr—played some bongos. George Harrison wasn't there. After fourteen takes, Lennon and McCartney did not make much progress.

Less than two weeks later, on June 1, the Beatles released the most recent album they had completed, *Sgt. Pepper's Lonely Hearts Club Band.* In only four years of recording, they had gone from the bouncy juvenilia of "Love Me Do" to the bleak sobriety of "A Day in the Life." The speed of their progress was staggering, unprecedented in pop music history, and likely never to be matched. After *Sgt. Pepper*, there was no imagining what the Beatles would do next, and what they did was return to the studio to work further on "You Know My Name (Look Up the Number)."

In the late 1970s, when I was just starting out in music writing, I interviewed the Beatles' producer, George Martin, by telephone from his studio in Montserrat for a minor article in *Rolling Stone* about production techniques applicable to home recording. While I had him on the line, I couldn't resist asking Martin about the Beatles song that baffled me most, "You Know My Name." He laughed when I mentioned the title and said, "Well . . . the boys adored the Goons—they could be very arch," and he said he had to go.

Indeed, it was a shared interest in *The Goon Show*, the satirical British radio and television program of the postwar years, that had provided an early link between the Beatles, then still a little rock and roll band out of the Cavern Club in Liverpool, and George Martin, a schoolmasterlike staff producer for Parlophone. Lennon, in particular, loved the brainy anarchy of the Goons, and Martin, before being assigned to the Beatles, had produced comedy records for two of the troupe's stars, Peter Sellers and Spike Milligan. "Their humor was the only proof the world was insane," wrote Lennon in a review of *The Goon Show Scripts* for *The New York Times* in 1973.

Picking up "You Know My Name" in three consecutive days of sessions, from June 7 through June 9, the Beatles—mostly John and Paul, with contributions from Ringo and, possibly, George—went full Goon. (McCartney is understood to be playing drums on some of the recordings, and there's no recognizable Harrison guitar on the released track, although, on one take circulating on bootlegs, Paul can be heard teaching George the chords.) Taking a whole new approach to the piece, essentially starting over, they cooked up a lounge-act cha-cha groove with piano, bass, drums, and maracas. The music was so different in feeling from the Four Tops–mantra material recorded earlier that the tape box for the day's work ended up being labeled INSTRUMENTAL—UNIDENTIFIED.

Overdubbing vocal parts, Lennon and McCartney turned the music into a piece of sketch comedy. John, playing a silky master of ceremonies, announces, "Good evening, and welcome to Slagger's, featuring Denis O'Bell . . . Let's hear it for Denny!"

McCartney comes in, as if walking onto the bandstand from the wings, and greets the imagined audience in a smarmy baritone—"Good evening . . ."—to a smattering of applause. With a few aural signifiers, Lennon and McCartney conjured a scene in a cheesy, half-empty nightclub, the sort of place where gray-faced old alkie swingers would cling to paltry remnants of the musical culture that rock and roll replaced. McCartney croons the title phrase, over and over, with impeccable unctuousness, ending every phrase with an overwrought vibrato. "You-*ah*, you-*ah*, you know my name, baby. You know my name—*that's right!*—look up my number. *Bah bah bah bum . . .*"

The character McCartney adopted, a caricature of a boozy Vegas-style entertainer, is so familiar to us now that it's nearly as much of a cliché as the brand of singer it mocked. Bill Murray, on *Saturday Night Live*, did an indelible take of this kind of entertainer as Nick Winters, cluelessly warbling wholly wrong material like "Scarborough Fair" and the *Star Wars* theme. The Muppets had their own felt-and-yarn version, Johnny Fiama; and Andy Kaufman, in his inimitable vein of psychodrama-comedy, brought an unsettling credibility to the lounge-act alter ego he created, Tony Clifton. At the time the Beatles recorded "You Know My Name," however, the only singers singing in the style McCartney ridiculed were doing it seriously. In 1967, a great many musical artists associated with the pre-rock era, such as Sammy Davis Jr., Judy Garland, and Mel Tormé, were still active presences in pop culture, appearing on the same stage as the Beatles, the Rolling Stones, and other rock musicians on TV variety programs like *The Palladium Show* in England. At the same time, a few younger performers, such as Engelbert Humperdinck and Vikki Carr, were making music grounded in the pre-rock style that played on pop radio stations and showed up on the charts.

"You Know My Name" is made up of five discrete movementlike sections, each recorded separately and later edited together. (Additional music was recorded and not used on the released track, including a ska vamp that can be heard on the extended, composite version of the song on the *Anthology 2* set released in 1996.) After the second part with McCartney's vocal, the music shifts to toe-tapping music hall bounce, and Lennon takes over, yelping like the music hall novelty-song star George Formby in a broad Cockney accent—"Yah know, yah know, yah know moy nyme." Echoing him in the background in a nearly identical voice, McCartney keeps time.

The Beatles were having great fun at the expense of their parents' music—in McCartney's case, almost literally, since his father, Jim McCartney, was an amateur musician who had played in community bands in Liverpool. Considering their history, this would seem considerably out of character for them. After all, the Beatles—particularly McCartney—had always been comfortable with vintage popular music and, in fact, performed Tin Pan Alley ditties, Broadway show tunes, and music hall numbers in their leather jackets and Cuban-toe boots in Hamburg. They played "Summertime" and "Red Sails in the Sunset" from 1935; they did "Your Feet's Too Big" from 1936, "September in the Rain" from 1937, and "September Song" from 1938. They clearly had enough regard for the better variety of old tunes to learn their complicated harmony.

As composers, moreover, Lennon and McCartney—again, Paul especially—showed an interest in historical song styles rare among rock musicians of the time. For *Sgt. Pepper*, a pastiche album in concept, the Beatles recorded "When I'm Sixty-four," an original tune of Paul's (begun when he had been sixteen years old and completed with John) that was indistinguishable from a sentimental ballad from the turn of the twentieth century. For the group's next project, *Magical Mystery Tour*, Paul would write a number in the same vein, "Your Mother Should Know," which the Beatles would perform in white ties and tails for television. Lennon, while later dismissive of this side of McCartney's output, calling it "granny" music, demonstrated how well he had absorbed Tin Pan Alley himself with "If I Fell," which begins with an old-style introductory verse and expresses a romantic sentiment with a lilting melody worthy of Irving Berlin. Lennon was also a devoted lifelong fan of Bing Crosby. At the time of his death, there was a jukebox full of Crosby's records in his New York apartment.

With "You Know My Name," the Beatles were doing multiple things in tension with one another. They were demonstrating both a fascination with the musical sphere of their elders and a degree of cheeky contempt for it. This stuff is fun to play, they seem to be saying, but even more fun to make fun of. There's no knowing their intent, of course—this is no more than a hypothesis—but it's possible that, by pointing out the ridiculousness of slick, second-rate nightclub acts, the Beatles were, in a way, proposing a defense of the integrity of music relegated to the fringes of the entertainment world.

In the fourth section of the song, "You Know My Name" takes yet another turn. After McCartney's singsongy countdown, there's a beat of silence, and then a tasty, swinging piano riff that sounds, to my ears, like something neither Paul McCartney nor John Lennon could have played. While I never had any trouble playing Beatles songs on piano as a teenager, I tried but could never quite get the hang of that part. The pianist on the track, a player with a clean, light touch and a strong feeling for swing time, vamps for a while, while a new voice (done by McCartney, I'm pretty sure) scats nonsense sounds—grumbles and harrumphs, coughs and growls, peppered with a guttural blurt of "Heavy, heavy!"—till the end of the record. The bit is, intentionally or not, a lot like the virtuoso comic "mumbles" routine that the jazz trumpeter Clark Terry had released on an album in 1966. On "You Know My Name," the bit is joyous, extremely funny, and slightly discomforting as a take-off on African American vocalizing.

The musical climax of the track falls right before the end: a simple but swinging alto saxophone solo played by Brian Jones of the Rolling Stones, whom McCartney had invited to the studio. "He arrived at Abbey Road in his big Afghan coat," McCartney recalled to Barry Miles. "I naturally thought he'd bring a guitar along to a Beatles session and maybe chung along and do some nice rhythm guitar or a little bit of electric twelve-string or something, but to our surprise he brought his saxophone. He opened up his sax case and started putting a reed in and warming up, playing a little bit. He was a really ropey sax player, so I thought, *Ah-hah. We've got just the tune.*"

On June 9, 1967, a master edit of the five parts was made by the engineer Geoff Emerick, and the tape sat dormant for nearly two years. It was not until April 1969 that Lennon and McCartney returned to the tune and finished it, adding more vocal flourishes and sound effects. "John and Paul weren't always getting on that well at this time," engineer Nick Webb told Lewisohn. "But for that song they went onto the studio floor and sang together around one microphone. I was thinking, 'What are they doing with this old four-track tape, recording these funny bits onto this quaint song?'"

In November of 1969, Lennon decided to have "You Know My Name" released—not as a Beatles record, but as the A side of a single to be issued under the name of the Plastic Ono Band, the project he had initiated in July of that year with the antiwar bromide recorded at a bed-in in a Toronto hotel, "Give Peace a Chance." The old Goon-inspired track apparently struck Lennon as avant-garde enough to fit in the resolutely outré image he was cultivating with Yoko. Test pressings were made, attributed to the Plastic Ono Band, and Lennon had Apple Records issue a press release announcing the record. The B-side was to be "What's the New Mary Jane," another offbeat recording with a repeated lyric—"What a shame Mary Jane had a pain at the party"—written by Lennon and recorded by John and Yoko with George Harrison at Harrison's home at the time of the

White Album sessions. When Paul and the other Beatles learned about Lennon's plan for "You Know My Name (Look Up the Number)," they had it canceled and decided to issue the song, at last, as the B-side of the penultimate single released while the Beatles were still together, "Let It Be."

I still remember the first time I played it—on my Sears record player in my room, with my best friend, Harry, when we were young teenagers. We knew "Let It Be" well, of course; it was a number one hit, and it had circulated on bootleg records for more than a year before its official release. We had come to expect surprises on Beatles B-sides—Lennon's wild "I Am the Walrus" had been the flip side of McCartney's "Hello, Goodbye," and Harrison's brooding "The Inner Light" had been the flip of McCartney's "Lady Madonna." But nothing could have prepared us for the loopy pranksterism of "You Know My Name (Look Up the Number)."

When the record was over, we stared at the turntable for a few seconds that felt like minutes, and each of us waited for the other to say something. Eventually, I said something to the effect that I thought it was the worst record I had ever heard in my life.

Harry took that in, and said he wondered if maybe that's what it was *supposed to be.*

I said something like *Oh, wow.*

And Harry, imitating McCartney's mumble routine, said, *"Heavy, heavy."*

HERE COMES THE SUN / THERE'S A PLACE

FRANCINE PROSE AND EMILIA RUIZ-MICHELS

I WAS IN MY TEENS before I even knew that the Beatles existed. That year—1962—an exchange student from the UK was staying at my family's house. The Beatles were already a sensation at home, so my Welsh friend was able to give me an advance warning about the tsunami of teenage mass hysteria that was soon to reach our shore.

As soon as I first heard the Beatles, I was a fan. I'd always liked the sound of voices singing harmony in thirds. Even as a child I'd loved gospel and bluegrass, but I'd never heard harmonies quite like those of the Beatles singing "She Loves You" and "If I Fell." Simultaneously unthreatening and hot, they were every adolescent girl's ideal, besides which they gave you a choice of which kind of guy you wanted to fantasize about. My friends and I talked about which Beatle we preferred: I was initially a George fan (I liked the spiritual type), but soon I changed my allegiance to John (I like witty bad boys).

I never screamed or wept the way other girls did. I never felt the urge to become part of a Beatlemaniac crowd. Mostly I remember listening to their first album, hour after hour, with the yearning accessible only to a teenage girl, listening to her favorite singers, alone in her room. Was John wondering what it would be like if he fell in love with *me*?

What strikes me now, and what many other members of my generation have written about, is that the Beatles grew up along with us. They took psychedelic drugs when we did, and *Sgt. Pepper* was born. The Beatles became interested in Eastern religion around when we did, though my friends and I were considerably more skeptical about the Maharishi Mahesh Yogi. The Beatles aged along with us, and John Lennon's death felt personal: a source of personal grief.

MY GRANDDAUGHTER EMILIA, who will soon turn nine, has been a Beatlemaniac for a little over a year. I can say this with precision, because it's Thanksgiving weekend as I write this, and it was last Thanksgiving that she watched the film *Help!* She played the title song so many times that by Sunday the rest of us asked her, begged her: Please stop.

Emilia's dad, our son Leon, is a musician, and at first he said that it was every musician's dream: to listen to the Beatles with your kid. But after we'd heard John cry out, dozens of times, that he needed someone, not just anyone, I think Leon began to rethink that. Basically, though, we're all delighted that Emilia likes the Fab Four instead of, say, Nicki Minaj.

Like me, and like a lot of our family, Emilia's a bit obsessive, and over time she's become something of a Beatles expert. I've heard her say, "Ask me something about the Beatles that I don't know." So far no one has stumped her. Asked to name a little-known fact about the Beatles, she says, "George Harrison's house had one hundred rooms." She's heard every song. She knows the lyrics to most of them. She knows who wrote each one, and on which album it appears. She's read eight books about the Beatles. She owns eighteen posters, all their records, and numerous photographs of them, alone and together.

This is how she remembers the way her love for the Beatles began:

"My parents were at work. And I was with my grandparents at their house. And my grandpa was playing 'Octopus's Garden' over and over again. Then he moved on to the next step. He played the White Album. I really liked the songs. Then, after my parents came to pick me up, my dad bought the White Album. The songs I liked best on the White Album were 'Rocky Raccoon,' 'Revolution,' and 'Back in the U.S.S.R.' The first two were written by John, and the last by Paul. Mostly, I like John's songs better, but it depends on the melody and the song."

Emilia's Beatlemania is, I think, purer than mine, less affected by history and time, more reflective of a child's love than a teenager's. I've asked her, as tactfully and subtly as I can, about "Lucy in the Sky with Diamonds," a song she greatly loves and about which we've had several conversations.

Thankfully, she seems to have no idea that the song has an acronymic relationship to a psychoactive substance.

She says, "The reason I like the Beatles is because I like the melody and the lyrics of the songs. And when my dad's away on tour, I like listening to the Beatles because they sort of remind me of him, because their music is a little like his. The music is something that my dad and I share." Emilia's Beatlemania *is* a musician's dream, or at least a musician's daughter's dream.

In a sense, my Beatles and Emilia's Beatles are different groups, different phenomena. I grew up with the Beatles— who were already quite old by the time Emilia first heard of them. So it stands to reason that we have different favorite songs.

Emilia says, "My favorite song is 'There's a Place.' I really like the melody. It's on the *Please Please Me* album, and it's not their most famous song. At first I thought that the lyrics didn't make sense, but my grandma explained them to me. And then I totally understood what John was saying. Sometimes when I am nervous or scared I think of happy things, like a dream I had once that I was getting a puppy, or once when me and Mommy and Daddy and my sister were in Italy and we found a plum orchard and started picking plums, and once when I went to the McCarren Pool in Brooklyn with my friend Lucy.

"Even though that's my favorite Beatles song—right now—there are others that I like a lot. I especially like 'I Should Have Known Better,' 'Help!,' 'P.S. I Love You,' and 'I

Want to Hold Your Hand.' I can play the riff from 'Birthday' on my guitar."

I'm intrigued by the fact that Emilia likes "There's a Place," because it often seems to me that the Beatles *is* a place where Emilia can go—a destination available to her for entertainment and pleasure, a refuge and a source of comfort when she feels any of the emotions that John is talking about: the desire for some respite and peace and good cheer when those feelings seem inaccessible. I've often been struck by the reality with which the Beatles exist for her. She's a regular kid, goes to school, has friends—but she also *inhabits* the Beatles and their world, almost as if they were characters in a novel, and she sees their situation and their life stories with what one might misidentify as an adult's empathy and awareness.

A year or so ago, we were riding in the car, and we heard John singing "Oh Yoko!"—his extraordinarily beautiful love song.

Emilia said, from the back of the car, "Can you imagine how John's first wife felt when she heard that?" I turned around, I suppose because I couldn't quite believe it was a seven-year-old who had spoken.

I know what Emilia means about "There's a Place," but it's not my favorite Beatles song. When I tell Emilia that "Here Comes the Sun" is the one I'd pick, she doesn't exactly shrug, but I can watch her attention skipping past and over what I've just said. Perhaps she thinks that this cheery, simple song is typical of her grandmother, whom she sees partly as a source of goofy positivity, lax behavioral standards, zero discipline, and periodic interrogations about what she's been reading.

So why *do* I so like that song? Maybe part of me remains that girl who liked George, the spiritual one, the one who looked a little like a saint in an Old Master painting. "Here Comes the Sun" has always seemed to me exactly like the message a believer might seek and hope to get from religion, any religion: the faith that the sun will yet return, shining brightly after the longest, darkest, coldest, and loneliest of winters.

Maybe it's also partly because I remember when and where I first heard it. It was the summer of 1969. I had recently arrived in Bombay, where the man I was traveling with had a fellowship to a local mathematics institute. I was in my twenties, emerging from one of those really bad years that young people have. I'd made the mistake of going to graduate school. I was uncertain about my future. Bombay was a revelation—a circus of color, light, and sound. There was poverty, certainly, but it was possible to live in South Bombay and not feel the poverty so intensely, just as one can now, in so many American cities. Every day brought some surprise that made me think that the world was a much more interesting place than I'd imagined.

A few weeks into our stay, we met an American couple; the husband also studied at the mathematics institute. They'd come better prepared, with a portable record player. Friends at home sent them new releases.

The first time we went to their apartment for dinner, they played us *Abbey Road*. I've never forgotten how happy it made me, how meaningful it seemed. "Here Comes the Sun" seemed like a personal message, written for me, the way good writing can. Winter was over, the sun had come out. Brighter days ahead. I loved the musical flourish that reminded me of the Baroque music I'd loved long before I'd begun to listen to the Beatles.

Or perhaps it's because one could say that it's the best children's song, ever. It may be too much of a children's song for Emilia at this point. In fact, it was one of the first Beatles songs she heard, but if the song's been omitted from her narrative of how she came to love the Beatles, it may be because she thinks her grandmother has claimed it.

I'm pretty sure that the first time we heard the song together was under the closing credits of a cartoon feature film about bees. I downloaded the song and we listened to it again and again, and talked about it together, conversations ostensibly about music and, beneath that, about the love that spans the generations.

LET IT BE

JOHN HOCKENBERRY

THE BEATLES SONG "Let It Be" is possibly the simplest song the Beatles ever produced. It is the only hymn the band ever wrote. Paul claimed it came from a dream about his dead mother. Aretha Franklin was actually the first to record it. John reportedly hated it and dismissed it as a bad Christmas carol. The album was supposed to be called *Get Back*, which made some sense. The lyrics in that classic rock song of a band getting back to where they once belonged seemed an obvious reference to what all of the band members were saying in those days. The studio had become too isolating. Something was missing. Live performance was something they yearned for if there was a way to avoid the insanity of the Beatlemania years that had caused each member of the band to withdraw from the world. But the Beatles would be no more. The break was clear to the band by late 1969, even if the world didn't know until two months after the single was released in March of 1970, followed finally by the album. Both were titled "Let It Be." There would be no getting back.

For years, "Let It Be" was not my favorite Beatles tune by a long shot. I was much more a fan of the studio wizardry in *Sgt. Pepper* and the White Album. By 1970, I had pretty much left the Beatles behind. The bubblegum live tunes felt dated, the most exciting studio stuff was coming from Stevie Wonder; Earth, Wind & Fire; and eccentric bands like Steely Dan and Weather Report. Billy Preston was listed as one of the musicians on the album *Let It Be*, but I preferred listening to him without a Beatles accompaniment. "Let It Be" seemed to be good musical advice. The Beatles were done. Let it be. And so I did, for forty years.

In May of 2010, my tall blond pre-teenager strode up to the stage for her sixth-grade talent show holding the cherry-red single-cutaway Guild six-string acoustic guitar I had bought twenty years before she was even born. I was more scared than she was. Olivia looked so alone in front of this audience of strangers. This was the very first year of her charter school. She was in the very first class. Where did her courage come from, this little girl who was so scared of the dark that she slept with the lights on and would never go upstairs alone? What was she even going to play? I had no idea. Our house was mostly filled with the refrains of Maroon 5, Katy Perry, and Lady Gaga. Eminem, Kanye, and Pitbull filled out the kids' playlists.

I had heard no rehearsing of a song even though my wife and I had been told that attendance at the talent show was mandatory. This was close to the end of a tough year for our family. Olivia had left all of her old friends behind when we were forced to take our four kids out of private school in 2009. Job loss, downsizing, shame, hardship, and just holding on—these were the icy steps on the rock face of those early Obama years, and my wife and I were determined to keep our kids on the right track, whatever that was. At that moment I was more than a little skeptical of this brand-new school, untested, our children's future buried somewhere in its zippy promises of "diversity," "excellence," and making "global citizens." Olivia was just eleven years old. The people in the auditorium were mostly strangers.

There was a whoop from the audience that broke the silence and unnerved me like a popped balloon. "Go, Olivia!" said someone else. Olivia shyly acknowledged both with a nod of her deeply blushing face and began to play in a breathtaking silence. They were simple chords strummed simply. I knew them. She sang the words. I knew them as well.

She sang out the words, lamenting a middle school student's times of trouble, calling out to Mother Mary, looking for the words of wisdom as though this song had been written for this talent show. Let It Be. The audience swayed as she sang haltingly at first, and then stronger. Everybody knew the song. She seemed so completely alone up on that stage, but black and white hummed and clapped and all were right there with her. I was overwhelmed with the courage it took for her to just walk up there, sit down, and sing like that. She wasn't doing some clever special arrangement of her own. She was playing the stripped-down hymn that John had made fun of and that Aretha understood instinctively, this calming religious revival song that symbolized the Beatles breaking up, but in that moment said we're together, let it be. The people in the auditorium joined in on the last chorus, which caused her to beam with a smile of such wonder and gratitude, it swept away all my anxieties about this school, these times, our insecurities, the big question marks that confronted our family now with a brand-new baby to go along with our two sets of twins.

When Olivia finished, the crowd was on its feet, shouting and screaming. I was shocked. My expectations about music and performance were exploded in that moment. I, who was raised in the hot-riffs, virtuoso world of my dad's classical and jazz training, was compelled to see the power and beauty of a simple song and its honest lyrics. The wisdom of "letting it be" could not have been more relevant in that moment, and I recalled clearly how the song had eased the mind of my seventh-grade self in a brand-new town and school after a sudden move in 1970. Forty years connected by a song that celebrated simplicity and a brave performance that reassured a father that the future was one step ahead, and then another, and another.

It was right then I understood why the Beatles are such a powerful force of art and music. Their body of work is huge and diverse, and yet this moment of hello and good-bye, as the Beatles were saying farewell as a band with this twelfth studio album while the world said hello to the 1970s, represents a huge turning point in popular music. The song "Let It Be" is the fulcrum on which all of the Beatles artistic invention pivots from the R&B early days of "I Want to Hold Your Hand" to the esoteric studio moments that gave us "A Day in the Life." The specific authorship within the personalities of the Beatles have always made a riddle of understanding their art. Add to that the influences of producers and collaborators like Phil Spector and Brian Epstein and the task becomes more complicated. "Let It Be" reminds us of the Beatles' reverence for song. Even though this is very much a McCartney track, you can hear the same simplicity and yearning for the clarity of song in John's solo work. "Imagine" is a good example of the kind of hymn he would probably have hated in the 1960s. George's "My Sweet Lord" is clearly from the same hymnbook if not the same religion.

As the heroic revolutionary 1960s tumbled into the muck and slime of the 1970s, we would say good-bye to the Beatles as a team, a concept, and a life force. They would become "artists." It was inevitable. Revolutions that contain the kind of collective up-from-nothing power that the Beatles delivered in those early days are never sustainable. Fans demanded deconstruction of this band into individual stars for worshipping. The John, Paul, George, and Ringo dolls were the start. Millions of dollars of licensed buttons and badges, toys and posters, bubble gum, and, my personal favorite, soda cans of official Beatle breath drove the Beatles phenomenon from a sound, to a band, to a brand—before decent people spoke of such things—to a quadraphonic personality cult. Ringo, Paul, John, and George were commercially extracted from this perfect ensemble long before we knew anything about them individually. We made them up in celebrity blips and rope-line moments while they receded into the shelter of the band.

IT COULD NOT STAY this way, of course, and just as the individual personalities of these four performers was revealed to us over time—John's genius and insecurity about being a real artist, Paul's perfect pop sound wisdom, George's pursuit of the ancient truths of an emerging counterculture, and Ringo, happy to be along for the ride—the band could no longer contain them. But unlike the Stones and the Doors or Big Brother and the Holding Company, the four musicians who made up the Beatles were in an inscrutable balance in their prime. The breakup of the band was such an emotional event for fans because it had no concrete, single reason you could point to. No Brian Jones flameout, or Jim Morrison/Janis Joplin tragedy, was there to explain the genius in its absence. The press blamed it on Yoko's influence over John, or they put it on George's interest in everything other than pop music. Paul, the one trained musician who really understood the whole pop music scene, was blamed for being greedy. He alone could make a solo career, and so he did, but there is little about it that resembles the un-earthly perfection of his band before Wings.

All of those reasons are correct and yet they say nothing about why the Beatles really matter, what we lost when they broke up, and why it all had to end. "Growing up" comes the closest, but it explains nothing. And unlike so many artists whose later work becomes whining psalms about how fame robs them of privacy and identity and makes a prison of their world, the Beatles never really speak of the conse-quences of fame in their work. There are all the playful jokes about fame in the movies *A Hard Day's Night* and *Help!*, but the films were quite separate from the music and the al-bums. In 1966, John got quite a reaction from religious Americans in the South and even KKK demonstrators from his suggestion that Christianity was in decline and that the Beatles were more famous than Jesus Christ. The band stopped touring after that. John looked back on this whole period in the darkly comic "The Ballad of John and Yoko" with a taunt to the religious right once again in the words "They're going to crucify me."

THE WHOLE CONCEPT of *Let It Be* the album was an argu-ment over how to play the music they had in essence in-vented. Was it better and truer to make their artistry in the studio as they had done with *Abbey Road* and *Sgt. Pepper*, with the complex electronic effects that they were pioneering, or to return to the stripped-down quartet sound that had served them so well in the early days of "Love Me Do" and *Meet the Beatles*? It was the first time in pop music that this issue of classic versus decadent, playing for the audience or for the artist, presented itself, even though such aesthetic arguments are thousands of years old. What is beautiful and tragic about the Beatles is that they should live this age-old conflict over artistic authenticity without really expressing an opinion about it. John's death arrested any evolution of the band's art into a partially finished canvas that can never be completed.

That in a song these four musicians should stumble on an answer to this question they never intended to pose is central to the Beatles' art and importance in world music. Songs from the album were played in a live performance with Billy Preston playing keyboards on a London rooftop in 1969. It was the Beatles' last live performance. It did not include the song "Let It Be," but the notion of leaving well enough alone hovers over the entire performance full of bad takes and restarts, which ended when the London Police told them they were violating municipal noise codes. Forty years later, that I should stumble on an understanding of the importance of leaving well enough alone while watching my eleven-year-old girl singing a song at her sixth-grade talent show suggests I should have given the Beatles more of a chance back in the sixties.

The Beatles recognized the enormous changes to come in the passive years after World War II and grasped those changes in the heroic sprit of wonder and the sardonic voice of skepticism that became the voice of youth culture at the end of the twentieth century. It all got away from them just as it got away from us, too. As we look back into the twentieth century for hints that can explain where we are now, we can see the Beatles and other examples of the solitary genius overtaken by waves of history. Our world seems so much larger, pulsing with uncertain urgency in these days. We await the new geniuses—we call them entrepreneurs now—who will deliver innovation or creativity (how many times have we heard those words?) or other miracles. We alight on the sparkle of the celebrities, the billionaire politicians and other messiahs, and yearn for them to make it all right. But as if foretold, it is only the Nowhere Men, the Fools on the Hill, and the Lady Madonnas who greet us. You get the idea. It will be a long twenty-first century.

MY DAUGHTER OLIVIA and her twin, Zoe, who was in the audience cheering her on, are both college girls now. I understand now why the Beatles would have found my children, why they would be more than just "Mom and Dad's music." Our family shows both the pride and the scars of coming of age. Our children find their own steps to take, just as a marriage must face the future ("When I'm Sixty-four") with children grown and youth gone with them. The Beatles stay with all of us. The lessons and bits of wisdom they gave us shine through the stained-glass windows from another century and comfort us.

Whispered words of wisdom: Let it be.

IT'S ALSO DECENT ADVICE as far as advice to parents goes these days: Let it be.

TWO OF US

BILL FLANAGAN

"TWO OF US" is the first song on *Let It Be*, the final album the Beatles released. By the time we heard it, in the spring of 1970, the song was already more than a year old and we knew the Beatles were disbanding. The group's breakup was addressed—mostly obliquely—in several songs they put out around that time: Paul's "You Never Give Me Your Money," George's "All Things Must Pass" and "I Me Mine," Ringo's "Early 1970," and, most directly, John's "God," in which he sang, "The dream is over . . . yesterday." At the climax of the medley on the second side of *Abbey Road*, Paul sang, "Boy, you're gonna carry that weight a long time," which might not have referred to the Beatles' dissolution but sure seemed to once we got the bad news.

But "Two of Us" had a different spirit. It was a nostalgic song, a look back at good times shared, with all the verses sung by Lennon and McCartney in harmony—the way we had come to know them in the first place—and a feature in short supply on the final Beatles albums. "Two of Us" ends with John and Paul singing, "We're on the way home, we're going home," and whistling off into the sunset like Hope and Crosby. It was how we wanted to remember them.

The song was written by Paul McCartney. From early 1968 until early 1969, Paul was on the hottest one-year hot streak any songwriter has ever enjoyed. "Lady Madonna," "Hey Jude," "Blackbird," "Back in the U.S.S.R.," "Helter Skelter," "Let It Be," "The Long and Winding Road," "Get Back," and more than a dozen others were written in that year. Even by McCartney's prolific standards, it was remarkable. It may have thrown out of whack the traditional balance between John and Paul. John had some great songs in that stretch, too—"Revolution," "Julia," "Don't Let Me Down," "The Ballad of John and Yoko" among them—but John was often focused on extra-Beatles endeavors. Paul picked up the slack, brilliantly.

McCartney has said that "Two of Us" was written about his new love, Linda Eastman. Linda had encouraged Paul to relax a little, not feel he always had to take responsibility for everything, and encouraged him to play hooky once in a while. They would go driving off into the countryside outside London until they got lost and then try to work their way home. "Two of Us" was inspired by those excursions with Linda, who Paul would soon marry.

That background does not change the fact that when Beatles fans, sad about the group's breakup, went to the movies to see the *Let It Be* film, they saw and heard John and Paul—looking as happy and brotherly as they had in

1964—sharing a song about the bonds of friendship that time could not break. It was a powerful and healing performance.

Of course, no song, no poem, no work of fiction, is about only one thing. The writer pulls from whatever is going on around him that helps fulfill the work. The lines "You and me chasing paper / Getting nowhere" seems more likely to refer to the business problems of the Beatles than the start of a new romance. Paul was falling in love with Linda as he was pulling away from his partnership with John. At the same time, John was pulling away from Paul to devote himself to Yoko Ono. Both marriages took place weeks after "Two of Us" was recorded. "Two of Us" is about the transition every person goes through as he or she gives up the old gang of pals to pair off with a permanent partner. The old two of us is making way for the new two of us. It's sad, it's bittersweet, and it's inevitable.

The album and film *Let It Be* had an odd history. In 1969, the Beatles owed United Artists another movie from the *Hard Day's Night/Help!* deal signed back in 1963. The later Beatles were a million miles from the smiling moptops of their youth, and there was no chance they would commit themselves to a scripted musical romp. (They did meet with Stanley Kubrick to discuss starring in a motion picture adaption of *The Lord of the Rings*; Kubrick told them the book was unfilmable.) Eventually the idea emerged to make a documentary of the Beatles writing songs, and rehearsing for and eventually playing a giant concert in a fantastic

destination. Among the suggested locations—an amphi-
theater in North Africa and a cruise ship in the ocean.

The project was provisionally titled *Get Back*. In January
of 1969, not long after completing the thirty-track White Album, the Beatles convened in a chilly film studio to take the
first step on this journey. It did not go well. The pressure of
having to continually top the Beatles was getting to John,
Paul, George, and Ringo. Working on new material with
cameras in their faces and soundmen documenting every
bum note and sarcastic comment did not help the vibe.
Ringo had quit the band and been enticed back during the
White Album sessions. During the *Get Back* filming, it was
George's turn to walk out. Apparently, something John said
to him during a lunch break—when the cameras were off—
was the last straw, but no one who was there has ever admitted to recalling what Lennon said. When John, Paul, and
Ringo resumed recording, John said, with characteristic
tact, "If he's not back by Tuesday, get Clapton in." Peace was
restored and George returned a week or so later with some
conditions—no more talk of a giant live show and no more
recording in a movie studio. Shortly thereafter, the *Get Back*
project was set aside.

The Beatles salvaged from the sessions a new single—
"Get Back"/"Don't Let Me Down"—released April 11, 1969.
A few days later, John and Paul went into the studio while
George and Ringo were unavailable and cut "The Ballad of
John and Yoko." In the summer, the whole band convened
for what would turn out to be the final Beatles album

recorded, *Abbey Road*. In the autumn, John told the others he wanted "a divorce," but the group agreed to keep it quiet until a new deal with EMI Records was completed. The others thought John might be in a mood that would blow over, as Ringo and George's resignations had.

But this time the split did not heal. There were business issues between the Beatles, musical and personal issues, too. Mostly, the boys had grown up. How long could the four most famous men in the world, men who could have anything by simply asking for it, swallow their pride and accept the criticism and vetoes of three old schoolmates when they went into the studio to make their music—the very thing that had gotten them to the top of the world in the first place? The Beatles had to end.

But it was tough on the fans. Great musicians and songwriters are like wise older brothers and sisters. They are a little ahead of us. They tell us what's around the next corner. Sometimes we don't like what they tell us is coming. I was fifteen when the Beatles broke up, when the shelved *Get Back* album was released as *Let It Be*, when the "Two of Us" clip was premiered on a special all-Beatles episode of *The Ed Sullivan Show*. I was just reaching the age when I could finally start living up to the example the Beatles had been holding up to us since 1964. Soon, I would be growing my hair, forming a band with my buddies, and taking cheap student-fare flights to London. The last thing I wanted to hear at that age was that my heroes were giving up the group to get married and settle down.

But of course, the Beatles were telling us the truth. There is a period in your life for running around, having fun with your gang, and then there's a time for finding your partner and having kids and building a family. The Beatles left us, but they didn't leave us alone. They left us with a map to follow. They showed us the way to go out into the world and get lost and they showed us the way to get back home.

ACKNOWLEDGMENTS

It was forty years ago today, or thereabouts, that I went to see *Beatle-mania*, a Broadway show advertised as a "rockumentary": *"Not the Beatles, but an incredible simulation."* I went four times as a kid, drawing mockery and more from my older brothers, who had not missed out on the real thing as I had. I think that the salt in the collective fraternal wound was when I bought the cast album.

How one can miss what one never knew, I don't know. But as I grew up, I felt as if I missed the Beatles, the way I felt as if I missed John F. Kennedy.

Yet while I regret not experiencing the Beatles in real time, I'm very grateful for all that they've given me, and so many others, starting with the presence of John, Paul, George, and Ringo themselves.

Special thanks to Sir Paul McCartney for contributing his personal note to this book. To Lee Eastman for making that possible. And to Steve Ithell and Lisa Power for their assistance. Without the inimitable George Martin, there would be no Beatles as we know them, and so we all owe him, for eternity.

The writers who contributed the pieces in this book did something sublime, spectacular, beyond what may be manifest. Aaron Sorkin once said, with regard to writing about Steve Jobs, "It's a little like writing about the Beatles. There are so many people out there who know so much about him and who revere him. I saw a minefield of disappointment." But the contributors navigated writing about the Beatles artfully, affectingly, in ways that felt all new. They wrote these pieces on planes and trains and in cars, wherever and whenever time allowed it in their lives. I hope that *In Their Lives* is a fitting tapestry of and tribute to the band.

The idea for the book germinated for a long time, and there were many moments along the way that led to its happening. One of them was in 2009, when then twelve-year-old Macklin Levine, on public radio's "This I Believe" segment, told her touching story of the Beatles, her father, and the lost family dog finding his way home.

This book would not exist were it not for several key people. Leslie Cohen was invaluable. I'm deeply in her debt, and indirectly, therefore, to the New York Society Library, without which Leslie and I would have never met.

At Blue Rider Press, I sent the original proposal for the book to the iconic David Rosenthal, who had the great gut instinct and wherewithal to give it to Becky Cole, who was pitch-perfect, an absolutely ideal editor. She in turn was aided, as was I, by Rebecca Strobel, who was a terrific asset to the project. Marian Brown, publicist extraordinaire, was aptly described by one of the book's contributors as "a beautiful soul." Ben Denzer did wonderful work on the book's jacket design, and Gretchen Achilles did the same for the interior. In my life as an agent, I'm so accustomed to hearing cavils about publishers, editors, publicists, et al., but here I have only praise and appreciation to heap upon mine.

Eternal, ineffable thanks to my family for indoctrinating in me a love of the Beatles, in the past, the present, and forevermore.

And then there is Jill. Jill Furman, for whom many of the Beatles' songs now seem to have been written. She has been a boon to this book and a blessing in my life. And Jill begat Sam, who just before turning two became a Beatles fan and who is a beautiful ballad and a propulsive rocker, rolled into one.

CONTRIBUTOR BIOS

THOMAS BELLER is the author of four books: *Seduction Theory, The Sleep-Over Artist, How to Be a Man,* and *J. D. Salinger: The Escape Artist,* which won the 2015 New York City Book Award for biography/memoir. His stories have appeared in *The New Yorker* and *Best American Short Stories,* and he is a regular contributor to *The New Yorker*'s *Culture Desk* blog. He teaches at Tulane University.

PETER BLAUNER is the author of seven novels, including *Slow Motion Riot,* winner of an Edgar Allan Poe Award from Mystery Writers of America, and *The Intruder,* a *New York Times* bestseller. His short fiction has been anthologized in *Best American Mystery Stories* and on *Selected Shorts from Symphony Space.* He has also written for several television shows in the *Law & Order* franchise and currently is a co-executive producer for *Blue Bloods.* His newest novel, *Proving Ground,* will be published in mid-2017. He lives in Brooklyn with his wife, the author Peg Tyre, and was a member of the Beatles fan club from 1966 to 1969.

AMY BLOOM is the author of three novels, three short story collections, a book of nonfiction, and a children's book. She knows most of the words to many Beatles songs. She has a novel coming out in 2017.

ROSANNE CASH is one of the country's preeminent singer/songwriters. She has released fifteen albums of extraordinary songs that have earned four Grammy Awards and nominations for eleven more, as well as twenty-one Top 40 hits, including eleven number one singles.

She is also the author of four books, including the bestselling memoir *Composed*, which the *Chicago Tribune* called "one of the best accounts of an American life you'll likely ever read." Her essays have appeared in *The New York Times, Rolling Stone, Oxford American, The Nation*, and many more print and online publications. In addition to continual touring, Cash has partnered in programming collaborations with the Minnesota Orchestra, Lincoln Center, San Francisco Jazz, and the Library of Congress. She received the 2012 SAG-AFTRA Lifetime Achievement Award for Sound Recordings and the 2014 Smithsonian American Ingenuity Award in the Performing Arts. She was chosen as a Perspective Series artist at Carnegie Hall and hosted four concerts (including a major show of her own in February) during their 2015–16 season. She also served as 2015 Artist-in-Residence at the Country Music Hall of Fame and Museum in Nashville. She performed three concerts there in September. On October 11, 2015, she was inducted into the Nashville Songwriters Hall of Fame. Cash's landmark 2009 album, *The List*, won the Americana Music Album of the Year award. On her latest release, *The River and the Thread*, a collaboration with husband, cowriter, producer, and arranger John Leventhal, Cash evokes a kaleidoscopic examination of the geographic, emotional, musical, and historic landscape of the American South. The album has received impressive worldwide acclaim and attained the highest debut in the *Billboard* charts of any of her previous albums. It received three Grammy Awards in 2015.

ROZ CHAST is the author of more than a dozen books for adults, including *Can't We Talk About Something More Pleasant?*, a *New York Times* 2014 Best Book of the Year, 2014 National Book Award Finalist, winner of the 2014 Kirkus Prize, and a winner of the National Book Critics Circle Award. Chast is also the author of numerous books for children. She is currently working with Calvin Trillin on a new book titled *No Fair! No Fair! And Other Jolly Poems of Childhood*. She collaborated with Daniel Menaker on *The African Svelte: Ingenious Misspellings That Make Surprise Sense* (2016). Chast grew up in

Brooklyn and received a BFA from the Rhode Island School of Design. She has provided cartoons and illustrations for nearly fifty magazines and journals. In 2013, she was inducted into the American Academy of Arts and Sciences. In 2015, she was nominated for the Eisner Award and received the Reuben Award from the National Cartoon Society. She also received the Heinz Award for her body of work. She lives in Connecticut with her family and several parrots.

SHAWN COLVIN won her first Grammy Award for Best Contemporary Folk Album with her debut, *Steady On,* in 1989. She has been a mainstay of the contemporary folk music scene ever since, releasing eleven superlative albums and establishing herself as one of America's greatest live performers. She triumphed at the 1998 Grammy Awards, winning both Record and Song of the Year for the top-ten hit "Sunny Came Home." Her inspiring and candid memoir, *Diamond in the Rough,* was published to critical acclaim in 2012. In 2016 she received the Americana Music Association's Lifetime Achievement Trailblazer Award.

NICHOLAS DAWIDOFF is the author of five books, including *In the Country of Country: A Journey to the Roots of American Music* and *The Fly Swatter: Portrait of an Exceptional Character*—a Pulitzer Prize finalist. He has been a Guggenheim, Civitella Ranieri, and Anschutz fellow, and contributes to *The New Yorker* and *The New York Times Magazine.*

DAVID DUCHOVNY is an actor, writer, producer, director, novelist, and singer-songwriter. He has published two books, *Holy Cow: A Modern-Day Dairy Tale* (2015) and *Bucky F*cking Dent* (2016).

GERALD EARLY is Professor of English and African American Studies at Washington University in St. Louis, where he also serves as the editor of the university's online journal, *The Common Reader.*

BILL FLANAGAN is a novelist (*Evening's Empire, A&R, New Bedlam*), a music writer (*Written in My Soul, U2 at the End of the World*), and a TV producer (*VH1 Storytellers, CMT Crossroads, The Breaks*). His essays appear on *CBS News Sunday Morning.* He wrote the liner notes for the

CD issues of the Beatles' Red and Blue albums and for the Beatles' *U.S. Albums* box set.

ADAM GOPNIK has been writing for *The New Yorker* since 1986. His books include *Paris to the Moon, The King in the Window, Through the Children's Gate*, and *The Table Comes First: Family, France, and the Meaning of Food*. A three-time winner of the National Magazine Award, he lives in New York with his wife and their two children.

DAVID HAJDU is the music critic for *The Nation* and the author of five books, including *Lush Life: A Biography of Billy Strayhorn; Positively 4th Street: The Lives and Times of Joan Baez, Mimi Baez Fariña and Richard Fariña*; and *Love for Sale: Popular Music in America*. He is also a professor at the Columbia University Graduate School of Journalism, as well as a successful songwriter, working in collaboration with Jill Sobule, Renee Rosnes, and Fred Hersch. In elementary school in New Jersey, he played rhythm guitar in a Monkees cover band.

JOHN HOCKENBERRY is the host of the nationally broadcast public radio program *The Takeaway*. He is a veteran journalist and author and has reported from conflict zones throughout the world. He has worked for ABC News and NBC News as well as NPR. Hockenberry is the author of *A River Out of Eden*, a novel set in the Pacific Northwest, and *Moving Violations: War Zones, Wheelchairs and Declarations of Independence*, a memoir of life as a foreign correspondent that was a finalist for the National Book Critics Circle Award in 1996. Born in Dayton, Ohio, Hockenberry grew up in upstate New York and Michigan, and attended both the University of Chicago and the University of Oregon. Hockenberry and his wife, Alison, live in New York City with their five children.

PICO IYER was born in Oxford, England, and raised in the fading Empire just as the Beatles were taking over the land. He is the author of a dozen books, among them *The Lady and the Monk, The Global Soul, The Man Within My Head*, and, most recently, *The Art of Stillness*.

CHUCK KLOSTERMAN is a writer and journalist living in Brooklyn. He is the author of nine books, including *But What If We're Wrong?*

ALAN LIGHT is the author of *What Happened, Miss Simone?*; *Let's Go Crazy*; and *The Holy or the Broken*. He also cowrote Gregg Allman's best-selling autobiography, *My Cross to Bear*. A former editor in chief of *Vibe* and *Spin* magazines, he is a frequent contributor to *The New York Times* and *Rolling Stone*.

REBECCA MEAD is a staff writer at *The New Yorker* and the author of *My Life in Middlemarch* and *One Perfect Day*. She lives in Brooklyn with her family.

RICK MOODY is the author most recently of *Hotels of North America*, a novel, and *On Celestial Music*, a book of essays. He writes about music regularly for *The Rumpus*.

JOSEPH O'NEILL has written a family history, *Blood-Dark Track*, and four novels, most recently *Netherland* and *The Dog*. He teaches at Bard College.

JON PARELES is the chief popular music critic of *The New York Times* and the consulting editor of *The* Rolling Stone *Encyclopedia of Rock & Roll*.

MARIA POPOVA is a reader and a writer, and writes about what she reads on *Brain Pickings* (brainpickings.org), founded in 2006 and included in the Library of Congress permanent archive of culturally valuable materials. She has also written for *The New York Times*, *Wired UK*, and *The Atlantic*, among others, and is an MIT Futures of Entertainment Fellow.

FRANCINE PROSE is the author of more than twenty books, most recently a novel, *Mister Monkey*. She is currently a Distinguished Visiting Writer at Bard.

EMILIA RUIZ-MICHELS lives in Brooklyn, New York. She is in the fourth grade.

ELISSA SCHAPPELL is the author of two books of fiction, *Use Me*, which was runner-up for the PEN/Hemingway Award, and *Blueprints for Building Better Girls*, chosen as a Best Book of the Year by the *San*

Francisco Chronicle, The Boston Globe, The Wall Street Journal, Newsweek, and *O: The Oprah Magazine.* Her fiction, essays, and nonfiction have appeared in a number of magazines and anthologies. She is a contributing editor at *Vanity Fair,* a former senior editor of *The Paris Review,* and a founding editor and now editor-at-large of *Tin House.* Schappell teaches in the MFA Fiction Writing Program at Columbia.

MONA SIMPSON is the author of six books: *Anywhere Here, The Lost Father, A Regular Guy, Off Keck Road, My Hollywood,* and *Casebook.*

JANE SMILEY is the author of novels, children's books, and nonfiction. She grew up in St. Louis, Missouri, went to Vassar and the Iowa Writers' Workshop, and now lives in California. Her novel *A Thousand Acres* won the Pulitzer Prize. Her most recent work is a trilogy of novels, Last Hundred Years. She teaches creative writing at UC Riverside.

TOURÉ is the author of *I Would Die 4 U: Why Prince Became an Icon* and *Who's Afraid of Post-Blackness: What It Means to Be Black Now.* His website is at Toure.com.

ALEC WILKINSON is the author of ten books, including *Big Sugar, A Violent Act,* and *The Ice Balloon.* Since 1980, he has been a writer at *The New Yorker.* Before that he was a policeman in Wellfleet, Massachusetts, and before that he was a rock and roll musician.

BEN ZIMMER is a linguist, lexicographer, and all-around word nut. He is the language columnist for *The Wall Street Journal* and former language columnist for *The Boston Globe* and *The New York Times Magazine.* He has worked as executive editor of Vocabulary.com and the Visual Thesaurus, as editor for American dictionaries at Oxford University Press, and as a consultant to the Oxford English Dictionary. He serves as chair of the New Words Committee for the American Dialect Society and organizes the selection of the society's Word of the Year. He was awarded the first-ever Linguistics Journalism Award by the Linguistic Society of America.